# Silent Moments

*When Your Present + Your Pleasure = A Future Unknown*

## Tammy Hinkle-Davis

ISBN: 1508706913
ISBN 13: 9781508706915

# Introduction

What you are about to read is a romantic drama that is going to take you on a mind-blowing, emotional roller coaster of passion, love, lust, guilt, shame, sin, fornication, and deliverance. You're about to enter into the world of Eva!

Eva is a woman who on the outside looks like she has it all: the perfect successful life, with the big house, the fancy cars, the ideal family, the great friends, and all the tangible things that come with it. Yet she is still searching for more. She has left the suburbs of St. Louis and has landed on Sin Drive, in the loft district of downtown, where every step she takes leads her away from the present, only to fantasize about her future.

The enemy has infiltrated her ideal life in an effort to destroy her purpose. But although she has stepped on the wrong side of town and out of the will of God, God still has a plan for her life. God continues to love her even in her mess, even when she doesn't love herself, and in doing so, He puts a twist of deliverance on her life.

We all know that when you are living in sin, the only end is destruction. But we also know that God can step into our life, and change our situation on a dime, and send us in a new direction. Changing our life and rerouting our end, so that we can live again, regardless of our present circumstances.

Even when you're in your most sinful mess, your suffering could be a part of your deliverance process. God can bless us how and when He chooses, if He chooses. And when God has a call on your life, you can rest assured that in the end, He is going to get the glory out of it, by any means necessary.

# Table of Contents

# 1

## The Call That Takes Me High

Another day I take this drive: speeding past traffic, my mind and body filled with anxiety. I've got the call, my ever-beckoning call. The call that makes my body burst with lust. I've been waiting and anticipating this call for days. It's funny because I knew that it would come; I just didn't know when, and that's what made it such a rush. My anxiety is rising, and my palms are sweating nervously, but in my mind I know I can relax now because I'm headed once again to the only place I can call comfort. I buzz myself into the lobby using those magic numbers that linger in my head like my favorite pick three (614), and I'm in. I take the stairs, anxious for what awaits me on the third floor. I'm blushing and smiling with flutter in my sway as if I haven't done this a thousand times before. Yet it always feels like the first time.

As I approach the door of comfort, I make sure that I'm all intact: my hair, my shoes, my sexy wind-flowing-jersey-knit maxi dress, and even my crisp, fresh aroma that exudes Light Blue throughout my entire body. I'm ready.

I knock on the solid steel door, although I know the door is slightly open, as it usually is, to let me know my eager feelings are mutual.

Echoes from my gold Gucci-studded heels echo on the hard cement flooring as I swagger into this Neo-Soul loft of love; I drop my purse and toss my keys onto the concrete kitchen counter as if I own it. This is my comfort. This is where I belong. This is where I want to be. This is where all my uncertainties are canceled and my heart is restored. Never having to leave here is my dream. This is my safe haven. I'm mentally home.

I'm looking for it. I'm wandering and looking, but trying not to look too obvious and/or adamant. I turn to the left, and through the frost that opens the doors to my heaven, I can see a shadow of it, the It that makes my mind and body feel free. Free of anger, free of pain, free of all the negativity that surrounds me every day. I can finally exhale. I see him. I see Love.

Drake greets me with a smile and big, bold, marble eyes that smother my heart with comfort as he approaches me. He is It. It is he. The man I love to love, but I can only love for moments at a time. He is my truth, my comfort, my heart. He is the energy that keeps me going, hoping that one day we will have much more than just a few hours to share and that we will no longer be loft lovers and that my true lover will no longer be a dream lover.

We hug and kiss, kiss and hug; we can't seem to take our hands away from each other. As he kisses me, the moisture of his lips feels like a sealed jar of fruit that has marinated in thick syrup juices for months, just to have me open the jar and be the first to savor every moist and juicy taste. By now my body is ready, as it normally is from his touch; my Lady Blues has turned into his lips. She is moist, she is wet; she is juicy and warm. Even before it happens, she can imagine him inside her and what is yet to come. She can't wait. He can't wait. Our moans and groans indicate that a week is too long, too long to have to wait for something that should be ours at will.

He raises my dress and notices that Lady Blues is not wearing panties, only to feel the moisture that covers his fingers like a warm, melting wax candle. In turn, I just close my eyes and let Lady Blues enjoy the moment, my head swaying from side to side, front to back, in an ever-so-high float. He is my high; he sends me to a place that only I know. It's him, it's the way he kisses me, the way he touches me, the way he shows just how much he misses me without saying a single word except, "Hey!" It's the way he looks at me, the way his eyes fall, like the sun going down on a cool autumn evening. This is everything that makes my Lady Blues sing. This is my fate, my destiny, and my future. Here is where my love resides.

He leads me through the frosted doors of heaven and lies me down on the all-white Egyptian-cotton sheets that feel like silk, under a cloud of cotton. I have arrived. I am here. I'm where I want and need to be. I'm once again in his arms and in his bed. He slides off my shoes, only to kiss my feet. He then stands me up and surveys my body, as if to let me know who's in charge. He has the control. I'm already weak. He slips my dress off, teasing me with his kisses and nibbles. He lies me down and then undresses himself. I lie there, touching myself to keep the Lady singing. One thrust and he's in.

"Oooooh, Eva! Oooooh…!" is all I hear him say with weakness in his voice. I'm in my heaven and my mind has stopped; all I can do is feel. I've become dizzy in his twirl of motion. I can feel his love way down deep, deep under my skin, deep down, down inside my soul. A shot of his soul has entered my soul; soul inside soul is the lovin' I'm feeling. We've made our connection. I'm addicted once again. His lips are attacking mine, and Lady Blues won't let me surrender. Lady Blues is hitting notes she's never sung before. She can't go on, but she doesn't want to stop. He's kissing and flipping and rubbing and touching me all at once. All I can say is, "Damn! Damn, damn, damn this man!"

The Man in the Hat is about to flood. I feel the strength growing in his thrust. Sweat and weakness enter his eyes. He holds my legs, feet against his chest. Thrust after thrust, it only gets stronger, and he only goes deeper. I can feel it. It's coming. I can't wait. He can't wait. It won't wait. I want it. I want it all. I want to taste it. I want to see it and more than that, I want to breed it.

"I can't take this, Eva!" he repeats with every moan, grunt, and thrust. I feel it; it's getting harder and harder, going faster and faster;

getting deeper and deeper. The Man in the Hat cannot go on. He has to let go. He releases, a burst of love energy that only we should share, that only I should be able to appreciate, because I do. I love him, I love it; I never want it to stop *coming*. Shoot it all out, and then spread it all over me. Massage my body with it. Then lie down and collapse in it.

# 2

## Hell of a Moment

The loud downtown traffic has awakened me, and the moment I dread has come again. I must leave my heaven and return to what is considered right at this moment to be my hell. How I want to stay, but I must go. My time is up. The dream is over and reality is starting to sink in. As I jump up in a panic, in disarray, searching for my bra, I hear it. It is the ring tone that haunts my life and it won't stop. It keeps ringing and ringing, like the annoying sound of a television station that has just gone off the air for the night.

A shock of fear enters my body, like a sharp bolt of guilty lightning.

"Damn! It's Malik." *Shoot!* I'm thinking. *How did I forget to turn my phone off?* Luckily, Drake had already awakened and was in the shower, because he would have gone bananas.

Drake knows that ring tone like it's his own ghost. He also knows that once the ringing starts, it will never stop until I answer. He knows that it's Malik and that he's more than likely looking for me.

Drake would then start yelling and screaming, saying stuff like, "Damn, it's bad enough I don't get to see you as often as I should. When I am spending time with you, I don't need your so-called husband calling, reminding me of my place. I don't know why he's calling anyway. Doesn't he know you're really where you want to be, or do you think it's time we tell him? Plus, I thought I told you to shut that damn phone off when you enter this loft."

Checking the mess out of me, in his reprimanding voice, after all the love we just made. To be honest I think he gets a kick out of it. It's his little way of condemning me for not getting divorced yet.

Oh yes, Drake will let me have it, if necessary. Drake is not just this charming, educated, amazing man, and my dream lover. He is also this; stern, head-strong black man who doesn't take any crap; from me or anyone else, for that matter. He barely wants to deal with this love triangle I have him involved in, but it's been too many years for us to turn back now, and we're too far gone.

"Shoot!" My cell phone is still ringing, but I can't turn it off, because if I turn it off now, Malik will know I've turned it off, so that's not an option. I'll just turn the volume down for the sake of Drake.

*Dammit! This pisses me off. Why does Malik do this to me? I just spoke with him three hours ago, right before I left work. I understand he's my husband, but it's like he's a weird stalker or something. I can never have a moment of peace. It's like he can feel me doing wrong,* I thought to myself while I'm still fumbling around looking for my bra.

By now the thought of Malik calling is driving me crazy, knowing he is probably still calling although I have turned the volume down and placed the phone in my purse to try to block it out of my mind.

My mind and body are already drained from the silent moment of passion I've just encountered with Drake, so I'm already in another place mentally, and now with this. My palms are starting to sweat, and this time is not from being eagerly excited; it's from fear. My mind is becoming disheveled with congested thoughts. I have to pull it together and think of something to tell Malik, about why I didn't answer his calls, and I have to think fast, but it's so hard to concentrate and think when everything is a distraction.

Like the sound of the water shutting off in the shower, which indicates that Drake is finished bathing and is on his way out. The fact, that I have yet to find my bra. The fact, that I'm fearful at the thought of walking out of Drake's door and saying good-bye, knowing it could be good-bye forever; not knowing if there will be a next time for us and if so, when. The fact, that I know my cell phone is still silently ringing inside my purse, and will never stop until I respond to it.

The Man in the Hat (aka Drake) is now standing in front of me, looking disappointed, wearing nothing but a towel. He stares at me with those big, marble, autumn eyes that have now turned down like blinds, as if to say, "I've seen this scene one too many times, and I'm tired of watching it: you trying to pull together quickly, grabbing for your things to ensure you don't forget anything, until you finally kiss me, then tell me that you honestly do love me and that you will see me later, and walk out the door. I know that once I close that door behind you, later may never come." This is how it goes each and every time.

It plays in his mind like a song, and it's written all over his face!

Drake just tippy-toes away from me; shaking his head in disappointment, leaving me standing in the middle of his living room; looking nervous and stupid with my bra, now in my hand.

And I'm thinking, *Man, I even love the way this man walks on his toes and gets upset. How did I let it get this far, and why is my husband calling me like this, dammit?* I glance at my phone and see nineteen missed calls from Malik.

*Ring, ring, ring,* nonstop. As I run quickly down the back stairs, leaving my comfort behind, leaving with nothing but all sorts of craziness running through my mind and a wet Lady Blues.

I question myself: *Do I have remorse? And if I do, does it matter? I am a mother, a wife, a lover, and a cheater; these are too many hats for one woman to wear. These weekly hours of passion with Drake, are they worth the risk of losing everything? And if everything did fall to pieces, would the Man in the Hat really be there to help me pick them all up?* If not, what a big price that would be for me to pay—not only for me, but also for my family and Drake as well.

It's always supposed to be the last time for Drake and me because in my Eva state of mind. *I'm disrespecting the most important institution that God created, which is my marriage; so I need to be an obedient wife and let Drake go.* But in my alter ego; E state of mind, I'm thinking. *How can it be the last time? How can I let go of someone that I love so dearly, like I love Drake—this is not just any old love affair, this is my refuge, my comfort, my hope.*

Because in my E reality, being with Drake is the only place I want to be, and I'm comfortable and secure when I'm with him, but in my Eva reality, I'm jeopardizing everything that God has ordained in my life, and all the hopes and dreams I have for my future will soon perish because of this sinful act of adultery.

It's a bit of a catch twenty-two: the moment I run down that back stairway to that hollow high-ceiling lobby and out that front door, hearing it slam behind me, I begin to count the seconds and the minutes till I'm back in that lobby, running up those same steps again, because I'm too scared to take the elevator for fear that someone may see me and recognize me, as an adulterous.

Only then, to go home to my kids, whom I love more than life itself; that recognizes me, as the perfect wife and mother; who honors and respects me, for who they believe me to be. To my home, where I fulfill my motherly duties and then fall asleep next to my husband, where I abandon my wifely duties, and dream of spending eternity with someone else and how happy I would be if Drake were to take Malik's place. Wow! Is this how I feel about the man I vowed to love and cherish, till death do we part, for better or worse? How could I feel like this?

The thought of one day waking up with a smile as I glance over and see the sweetest thing, my lover, my man, and my best friend, Drake; the man who I think was made especially for me, my soul mate, my homeboy, my partner, my friend; Drake, the man of my dreams. That for now can only be a dream.

*Ring, ring, ring,* nonstop. I can barely get in my truck, I'm so nervous. I have to prepare myself before I answer, because I can't answer now; I'm not fully focused yet. I have to take a minute to get my thoughts and lies together.

So I'll just let it ring, and I'll call him back in a second, once I pull it together.

While dialing Malik back, I notice that my palms are still sweating, and now so is my forehead. I fear the conversation and what I'm going to say this time...

But even before I can think, before he even picks up the phone, guiltless lies flow through my mind and roll off my tongue, right in the nick of time. He picks up without saying a word. All I hear is silence, but I know he's picked up because the phone is no longer ringing. So I begin to speak.

My voice stays strong and confident, with no stutter.

"Hello! Hello! Hey, baby, what's up? I was at the mall; I see you've been calling me. What's wrong is everything OK? Are the kids OK? I tried to call you back to see if you needed anything after I spoke with you earlier when I was leaving work and headed to the mall, but my phone couldn't get a signal." *The key is not to let Malik speak before I'm done speaking, so I continue,* "What's going on with you? I'm en route home." There's still a silent pause. *Shit,* I'm thinking, *say something; I need to know your location and position before I say another word.*

Malik finally speaks. "Eva, I've been calling you for over an hour," he says with frustration in his voice. "So you're telling me you've been in the mall all this time, since you left work?"

"Yeah, baby. You know me and the mall, plus I told you, every time I tried to call you, my signal would fail. I didn't even realize you had called until I got back in the truck, that's when all my texts and calls started coming through, and of course I had several missed calls from you. You had me panicking for a minute; I couldn't call you fast enough, once I start seeing all your calls and texts come in." *This helps to calm him down, as well as reconfirm my lie.*

"E, weren't you just at the mall a few days ago? Man, you gone put us in bankruptcy court; just get home, we'll discuss it then, and did you get any food for your family at the mall? I have already picked the kids up, and we are hungry and on our way home. It's going on seven o'clock. You, that mall, and especially that phone drive me crazy."

Bingo! I wiped the sweat off my forehead and felt my palms drying up. I now knew his location and position. I could start breathing again.

He had the kids and was on his way home, and his voice didn't sound as frustrated anymore, just hungry and irritated.

"Well, baby, since I'm just leaving Von Maur and that's about forty-five minutes out, I thought I'd just stop and get something. I knew it would be too late for me to cook when I got home, and bringing food from the mall would not have been good. Tell the kids Mommy said hi, and I'll be home in a few. Love you guys." *This will buy me some time to pull it together since Malik knows how long the drive is from Von Maur to the house*, I thought.

"OK," he says in a nonchalant tone and hangs up. I wipe my forehead again, give a little mischievous grin, and hang up too, thinking, *Damn! I cannot keep doing this. Something has got to give.*

After hanging up with Malik, I just sit in my truck in Drake's parking lot, staring off into space, thinking, *This is my husband, my life, my family. What am I doing, and why can't I stop?*

I then pull down the overhead visor and look into the mirror to check my makeup and make sure my hair doesn't look like quickie-sex hair and I notice a stranger looking back at me.

A face filled with lies and deceit is looking right at me in disappointment. So I just stare back and ask this stranger, "Am I living for the possibilities of what could be? Will Drake and I ever be, and are we even really meant to be, or should I stop tripping and let Drake go?"

I shake my head in dismay and then take a second glance back into the mirror, hoping to get the answer. But this time I don't see a stranger with a face full of lies and deceit. I see a face full of baggage. My face. The face of a woman who's carrying around a bag of hurt and dreams, hurt from my husband and his deceitful ways, and dreams that only appears realistic for a few hours a week with Drake.

A woman who has a vision of happiness that lies sadly in her eyes and with another man because of a husband who has ruined the possibility of me ever loving him again. So I think to myself...

*This vision only appears, when you feel you've found something or someone who makes you feel completely worthy; someone who is able to fulfill your entire dreams with just his presence and conversation; someone who makes your heart feel safe and secure. Safe enough to hand your heart right over to him and secure enough to know that it's in good hands and will be OK.*

Then I had a love-struck-confused Drake moment...

*What's funny about my heart is that right now, it doesn't understand patience. It doesn't know the difference between hours, days, or weeks. It lives for the moments and reacts to how it feels during those moments. My feelings for this man have changed everything and right now my feelings are my truths... Or am I just a sucker in lust, who can't tell my feelings from my distractions and the truth from a mirage?*

Could this be a big fat web of lies that has me all entangled; and if so, how do I loose myself? *What have I gotten myself into?*

It's so unfortunate and such a shame that I have to live a lie to steal heartfelt, silent moments with Drake to get the fulfillment and feelings that my husband can no longer provide for me because of his past infidelity and indiscretions. But does it make what I'm doing and what I feeling for another man right?

# 3

## I Fault Hubby

I pull into the garage, being sure to do another glam check, making sure that everything is intact, just the way it was before my encounter with Drake a few hours ago. Of course, I've stopped and picked up something for dinner just as I told Malik I would do. I may be a cheater, but I still try to be a good wife...in my, he-he-he laughing voice.

I also had to cover my behind and make a quick stop at some over-the-top expensive, shoe boutique by the house. Hell, he's a man. He won't know where the shoes came from, plus, I'm not keeping them anyway. These are just being used as a camouflage for today; this can be a reason for me to have another Drake mission next week. LOL! *"Babe, I was taking those shoes back I purchased last week. They were too expensive, and plus they hurt my feet"*... another he-he-he laughing moment.

I just knew that I could not walk in this house empty-handed, without a shopping bag, new shoes, or something, considering I told him I've been at the mall during the time I was on my Drake mission. That would have opened a whole other can of jokes, except Malik would not have been he-he-he laughing with me, and the joke would have been upside my, he-he-he head. (OK!)

I greet Camilla and Cameron, my darling children, with a smile, kisses, and hugs as I walk through the garage back door, into the kitchen. To help calm my paranoia, I start a conversation. I ask them how their day was at school and if they have any homework. Their response is just as normal as it is any other day, so at this point I haven't picked up on any red flags. I might just be home free and in the clear zone.

As I sit the food on the counter, I ask them, "Where's Dad?"

"Dad's upstairs watching the basketball game," Camilla says.

Not to look guilty, I flip off my shoes and start up the stairs to follow my everyday routine, only to be undressing for the second time today.

"Hey, baby!" I say with confidence as I reach the top of the stairs while walking toward him as he sits in his favorite chair watching his favorite sport, basketball. "Who's playing and who's winning? I got Chinese: shrimp egg foo young, your favorite. It's all downstairs if you're hungry. We're all about to sit down and eat in a minute. Cameron already has the game on in the kitchen so you can watch it down there." I lean over, attempting to give him a kiss on his lips that lands on his cheek when he turns away.

I can sense suspicion in his eyes just from the way he watches the television with no enthusiasm as if his mind is somewhere else, and I definitely feel it in the cheek kiss he gave me. I just stand straight up and say, "Bad night? Your team must be losing." *As if I really care.*

In the back of my mind, I am thinking, *Oh well, I don't care what's going on. I'm good. You can bring it tonight if you want to, 'cause I'm ready!* That long drive home had built up my courage and cockiness. Since I had picked up the food and had a shopping bag with new shoes in it, I was safe. Plus, the video recorder in my mind kept replaying flashbacks of the Man in the Hat and all that good lovin' and magic love potion that was just released all over my body. So, I was good, on both ends.

Then just like that...

From that instant thought of where my body and soul had just been, my state of mind is at ease, and my bring-it-on, I-don't-care attitude is now relaxed. It's amazing how just the thought of Drake brings calmness to my spirit. *Whoo!* I thought, *This man shool got a hold on me* in Madea's voice, 'cause the only bring-it-on attitude I now have is thinking about next week, when it's time for Drake to inject Lady Blues with some more of his love antidote. Damn, damn, damn, that man.

I'm good, my kids are fine, dinner is on the table, once again I've managed to somewhat outwit my husband with my sneaky, con-artist ways that I learned from him, so no matter what he's thinking right now, it would be foolish of him to act on it; especially in front of the children. Plus, that's not his style anyway. He'll just wait until tomorrow and drink all his concerns away with his boys, like he always do on Friday nights, Saturday night, Sunday nights, and any other night he feel like drinking and staying out all night.

All I want to do right now is bathe in a tub of Laura Mercier, lie down, and reminisce about today, and dream the dreams that nourish my soul and keep me going until next week. But guess what? I can't.

I have to be the wife and mother I vowed to be years ago. I have to play this game of wifey all the way until the end. Until all the cards are turned. One bad move on my behalf tonight; and it will be a long night. I may be calm, confident, and feeling safe 'cause I'm still flying high off of drug Drake, but I'm no fool.

So I will chalk up bathing in Laura and relaxing as a loss and just go into the bathroom, act as if I'm constipated, clean Lady Blues up with some wipes real good, put on my robe, and head back downstairs. I'll fix my family's dinner plates and possibly be able to take a bath later—that is, if Malik isn't still walking around looking like Colombo, suspiciously looking for clues, to catch me off my square.

If all else fails, I'll just go to bed wearing Potion La'Drake all over my body and wait to take a bath in the morning. But for now I must go on living the life of a well-to-do wife and mother: snap back to reality and view this whole day as a summer's rain.

*You can always smell the rain even before it comes, and you dread it because it's sure to ruin your plans. But after the rain the sun always rises, and if it weren't for the rain providing nourishment to produce the flowers, there would be no beauty at all. My husband is my rain, my children are my beautiful flowers, and yes, Drake, he is my sun. The sun is what brightens up the gloomy days. Just when you think it will never stop raining and the sun will never appear, it just pops up out of nowhere, and you forget about the rain altogether. Then you realize that waiting out the storm wasn't all that bad because you're so delighted to see the sun, and the sun even brings along a rainbow as a little added bonus.*

We sit down at the dinner table and begin to bless the food. While everyone else is blessing the food, I'm praying to God that my husband doesn't want any sex tonight because it would be just my luck if he did. That would be the crusher for the day, because tonight; *It won't happen.com* in my Tamar Braxton voice.

Sorry, Malik, but it won't!

After dinner is over, I'm trying to find anything to do to keep from going to bed while Malik is still awake. I mean, it's serious: I can't even get in the bed and watch television. I have to stay as far away from the bed as possible because, man, I have really messed up the Drake/Malik rotation. It has been days since Malik and I have had sex. Why did I let it go that long? Normally I have it spaced out to give me, no more than three days in between, and this week I've tripped. So, I know it's bound to be an issue tonight for Malik. But even with that, this would be a typical Malik reaction, since I've been missing in action for a few hours today. I can practically read Malik's mind; I know exactly how his little insecure mind thinks.

"Oh, so she says she's been at the mall all day today; yeah, well, we'll see. She ain't had sex with me in four days, so we will see tonight. I bet she better be fucking me tonight." Yes, that's Malik, Little Mr. Insecure, got to prove a point with sex. Can a woman just be tired? Damn! Normally, I'd give him some really good head and go to bed, but even my jaws are not in the mood tonight. They tired too.

The longer I walk around trying to find stuff to do, the more I can sense his curiosity building up. See, I know my husband. So, I have got to go to bed soon, and this is sooooo not funny because I still smell like Potion La'Drake under the surface and probably taste like it too.

The kids are asleep now, and the kitchen is all clean. I've been on the computer since the kids went to bed hours ago; I cannot stall too much longer on this computer because in a minute that's going to open some more drama doors; he's so insecure, he'll think I'm on BlackPeopleMeet. com or some crap like that or having cybersex with someone I've never even met on Facebook.

I have enough going on already, without Malik running around playing Chris Hansen on *To Catch a Predator* with me. But that's just how he thinks; he has done so much dirt, he done jacked his own mind up.

It's getting later and later, and I have got to go to bed, but I have to figure out how I'm going to do it without giving up the booty. *Should I take my journal to bed, and act as if I'm writing?* That's a thought!

So I slip into the room as quietly as I possibly can, thinking Malik would be on his way to sleep, if he's not sleep already. Then I notice Malik's ass lying there, naked—naked as a newborn baby. I mean, just lying there, with nothing on.

I can't tell if he's asleep or dead, because he's just naked and not moving. *This is bananas*, I think. I just look up at the ceiling as if to plead with God. *God, don't do this to me, I will do better; you know my heart, you have got to be kidding me! I paid my Tithes on Sunday. Even though I didn't go to church and haven't been in a while, I still gave them to Nyla, and I paid extra. This cannot be happening. Any night but tonight, Lord…I know he's my husband and I am not supposed to deny him and all that marriage biblical stuff, and I know I haven't been acting like the perfect wife here lately. But you know I'm going to get it together before it's too late, please, Lord, not tonight. Give me a break tonight…Amen!*

I'm hoping and praying that Malik's asleep, and if he's not, he's just lying there naked as a jaybird because he's hot and/or too tired to put on his pj's—just as long as he's not hot in need of me and I hope, that he's too tired to even fathom it, 'cause that would not be good for either one of us.

I have had a wonderful day, and I don't want it to end like this. Besides that, I'm sticky, smelly, and not only is La'Drake all over my body, but it's also injected all up in me, too! Not only that, but after the shakedown that went-down, on today with the Man in the Hat, Lady Blues is a bit sore and would be devastated if someone else tried to bust in the party, disturbing the groove from earlier.

She's already upset because she didn't get a chance to take that long, hot, Laura Mercier bubble bath to rejuvenate her, so she's still in remission. So don't start none, Malik, won't be none; in that order.

Now my thoughts have gotten me angry!

It's amazing how a few hours of personal pleasure can alter the rest of your day. You see, I don't want to pull out the drama cards on Malik's behind tonight. I just want to relax and enjoy my thoughts and drift off to sleep with my cheating, selfish self. LOL.

But for real, *I don't want no drama tonight…and curiosity killed a cat; so Malik better be careful.*

Now, if Malik pushes the envelope, and I must pull out the cards, then out they will come, but I would prefer to avoid all that. See, there are a few things Malik always fails to remember in this marriage, and that is that he has faults too. Way more faults than I have. You see, I don't consider my situation with Drake a fault. I consider it a forced choice—something I chose to do forcefully, because I felt that during the time when Malik and I were legally separated, it was my prerogative, after all he had put me through. Therefore, he forced me into another man's arms.

And one day, I truly believe that Drake and I are going to make it official; it's just that, right now is not the right time for us. There are still things that need to be worked out between Malik and I, like our kids, who right now need both parents in the household. Unfortunately, the other parent happens to be my husband and their father, and a sneaky, conniving, cheating, drunk, but it is what it is.

It's not my fault that I just happened to have found the man of my dreams, my soul mate, the man who I believe, was made especially for me; later in the game, while being married to Malik. If it wasn't for his infidelity and our separation, none of this would have happened.

Sometimes I think you meet seasonal people to help you grow, and to go through things with; you know, as a helper, someone to help prepare you for what is to come. But once you've completed that season with that helper, it's time to move on and fulfill your own destiny and happiness. That is what I think has happened in my situation with Malik; his season has passed, but because we have children together and are married, we can't move on just yet. Therefore, we have to deal with each other until we are forced to do something different.

I would like to think that Malik was my stepping-stone and breaking ground for love because he caught me when I was young, number one; I was vulnerable, number two and I was naïve and didn't know any better, number three.

I was just looking for a man to take care of me, that's all, no more, no less. You know; the daddy issues syndrome that most young women have, 'cause mine wasn't in the picture; I was just a little girl looking for someone to fill that void, and then one day Malik came along to rescue me.

Yeah, that was me.

He was perfect; I mean, the man was over ten years older than me, established, had money, and wanted me. I was just a kid, and he was a grown man. I didn't really think much about us having a future together, all I thought about, was how convenient it was at the moment. But now I feel like it's time for me to move on and live my life, not out of convenience but out of love. I haven't figured it all out yet with the kids and all, but I'm working on it.

Malik has put me through a lot these past few years, and I've still stood in the position of his caring, supportive wife; through it all, enduring much pain but still standing. His faults have surpassed mine tremendously. To tell the truth, I don't know why I didn't leave and stay gone forever, but again, I had to think about my kids.

You see, Malik shit is raggedy and messy. As a wife and mother, I just play my role and sometimes let things slide and play the fool (emphasis on *play*), but never forgetting, just forgiving because of our children—just storing all that extra mess that Malik has done in our marriage and to our marriage away, in the back of my mind, just for moments like this one.

Not to use them in any way as a crutch or a reason to have my weekly hours of passion with Drake, because that is beyond reason. *Now!*

Malik's mess is my just-in-case ammunition. That's what I like to call it; it has nothing to do with Drake or anything else, 'cause right now, I feel like, Drake is my solution and my answer. See, in my mind, body, and soul, I am Drake's lady and he is my man. We are playing the roles of a down-low couple for now; just sitting back, and waiting for the right moment to come out of the closet.

Nothing and no one can change what we have but us, and only we understand our situation and where it is headed. Only we know our plans. No one else has a clue. What was that song from back in the day? "Secret Lovers"—yeah, that's it, that's what we are for now. And for now, I'm cool with that. At least I have enough respect for my family, that my dirty laundry ain't being aired all in the streets of St. Louis like Malik's. And the funny thing is that he really thinks that I don't know; that I don't hear things, that I'm still his little, young, naïve angel. Huh!

So this is all the more reason why I'm going to get into this bed and have no problems out of Malik; and if I do, I'm prepared to go there and pull out my just-in-case basket full of dirty laundry ammo, on his ass.

# 4

## Sex Switch & Spin

*I* ease into bed. Instead of writing in my journal, I put my iPod plugs in my ears, pull my sleeping mask over my eyes that read, "Diva at Rest," and pray once again that it's a done deal and that Malik's asleep. They say the third time is always a charm. I guess that's a lie; three times, wasn't good enough. *For the love of Jesus!* Not even ten minutes later, Malik starts. I barely lay my head down on the pillow and get comfortable, before he is up and at it.

"So, I guess this will be another night I go without fucking my wife!" he says in a disgusted tone of voice.

*Oh hell no*, I say to myself. *Did he just say fucking his wife? Yes, he did.* I lie there quietly, listening to Sarah Vaughan, trying not to feed into any of his nonsense.

So, I act as if I have already dozed off and didn't hear a single word he said, knowing this would not work, because we've been through this time and time again. But I still continue to lie there, hoping that this time it will go a little different, considering he's not drunk. But lo and behold he just continues to go on and on with his grunts and sarcastic gestures. That would normally piss me the hell off immediately, but tonight I'm in another state. A state of mind, that is, and I will not let him interrupt my dreamy thoughts that are now visiting paradise through the sounds of Dinah Washington and dancing to "What a Difference a Day Makes " with Drake.

Then all of a sudden out of nowhere, Malik snatches off my mask. I want to say, "Didn't your dumb ass read the sign," but I just look at him like he is crazy. I'm thinking that by looking at him in this manner, it will intimidate him and make him lay his ass down and stop the bullshit, but of course it doesn't. One thing leads to another, and before I know it, the shit hits the fan.

I really don't feel up for this shit tonight. I really don't feel like pulling the drama cards out on his ass, but I should have known if I wasn't giving up the ass, there would be repercussions. As I pull the iPod plugs out of my ears, I think, *Ass or repercussions, repercussions or ass? What do I do now? Do I dance to his beat and fuck twice in one day without taking a bath? Or do I go there, on his ass? Hmm…*

It only takes me a second to dignify that question with an answer and that answer is, *Oh hell no. Fucking is not an option.* That's some nasty shit; considering I'm swarming in massage oil called La'Drake (Drake's come)! Instantly I decide; *I'll take repercussions for one hundred, please.* I'm going to dance to my own beat, so fuck it; let the games began.

I jump up, turn my iPod off, and slam it on the nightstand; my dreamy trip to paradise is officially over.

"Look, Malik," I say in a rather aggravated tone. "I don't know what the hell you're on tonight, but I'm not for this bullshit. Just because you've finally found your way in the house before the a.m., don't think I should be all laughs and giggles, as if you've done me a favor. I'm tired. I've had a long day at work today, and besides that, I'm constipated and I'm PMSin'. So I would advise you to step off and leave me the hell alone. I'm trying to be an adult about all this shit for the kids' sake, but for real I'm barely two seconds off your ass. As a matter of fact, I got a question I need to ask you anyway…

"Why don't you go fuck that bitch who had yo black ass out until three in the morning last night? While you waking me up and shit, how about you go wake her ass up? I bet that ho ain't losing no sleep. That bitch probably got on a snuggle on somebody's floor, dreaming about you and what a good time she had with my husband last night, but unfortunately me, the wife, is at home arguing with her husband in the a.m. about BS and another bitch.

"I tell you, typical; the wife has to put up with all the bullshit, but the ho, just go on about her business peacefully with a wet ass. I swear, Malik, once again you've started this same old shit; and oh, don't stand there looking confused, because the only confusion is what time you think you can walk into this house without it being a problem.

"You know the shit I'm talking about, Malik, the same shit that had your ass living alone a few years ago. I don't even know who you are anymore. You stay out all night; you come and go as you please. Then, when you finally come home from being out all night, your draws are on backwards, and you are so drunk, that you don't even know where you are; you're just lucky to have made it anywhere without wrecking another car.

"You're not spending time with the kids, and think that if you pick them up from school, you should get an Achievement Award. This is the first time in weeks you've actually been in the house before midnight. I don't know a man on this earth who leaves home at eight in the morning going to work and comes in after midnight the next day. If you stay out past midnight, why not stay out until eight and make it a whole twenty-four-hour shift, and tell that ho to cut you a check.

"So, while you got the nerve to be waking me up in the middle of the night, asking me for some ass, knowing your ass should be on sex restriction for the rest of your life. You need to be asking for some forgiveness and a watch. You might just be lucky enough to get the watch; apparently you don't have one, because you can't keep up with the right time to enter my house, nor do you have any respect, coming in my house with your draws on backwards, since we're going there! Walking in here like it's all good; improperly dressed, all hours of the night. Even if you don't have a watch, yo ass is black, so I'm sure yo mama taught you, that when it gets dark, and the streetlights come on, it's time to bring yo black ass in the house and I'm *sure*, she taught you how to put your draws on.

"And as far as forgiveness goes, once again it's gradually evaporating. My forgiving days are just about to be over for you. You have drained me dry, and I'm getting too old for this shit, Malik."

He just looks at me, eyebrows all in a bunch, and says, "What the fuck was all that shit you just said to me, and where the hell did all of that come from?"

"You heard what the fuck I said, Malik, all ninety-nine hundred words of it. Oh my bad, I'm sorry, I forgot. I know if you can't tell time and don't know the difference between the front and back of your draws or when it's time to come home, you're probably having comprehension issues with everything else. Or maybe you are still drunk from several years ago; I don't know. But what I do know is that you are an alcoholic, and your body will never fully be sober 'cause you're constantly drinking every damn day, and you know you're diabetic. *Who does that!*

"But in regards to screwing you, let me break it down for you in a language and tone that maybe you can understand a little bit better: *Go screw that bitch who keeps you out all night!*" I screamed the last part at the top of my lungs, so loudly that I thought I might have awakened the kids and the neighbors.

"Eva! I don't need a bitch. I could care less about a bitch, and I'm working on my drinking; I'm not and alcoholic, my physiatrist said it's a disease and it will take time. And why you got to bring up my illness? And that underwear thing; let it go Eva, I'm talking about my bitch and why she ain't fucking me!"

"Oh hell no! Did you just call me a bitch? Yeah, I'm a bitch all right, a bitch that's about to go berserk on your black ass! Bitch, huh! Yeah, I got yo bitch!"

In a matter of seconds I had went straight hood on his ass, walking and pacing the floor like a mad black woman in a Tyler Perry movie, trying to think of what to say next. He just stands there in a state of shock, looking like, *OMG! She about to kill me. I done messed up now.*

"Oh, OK, Malik, I see you wanna play the name-calling game, the stay-out-all-night game, and all those other Malik games you like to play. Well, guess what game this bitch ain't gone play tonight. This is one bitch that ain't playing the fucking game tonight and no other night at the rate you're going. I'm the bitch that's about to go sleep on the couch before I have to kill your disrespectful ass...*just disrespectful*, for no reason. And Lord knows I don't have time to be going to jail for no petty, kill-a-husband shit like this. I've seen *Snapped,* and it never ends up in the woman's favor. Just because I'm tired and don't feel like fucking tonight, you wanna call me a bitch. Not worth it. Fuck you, Malik. I don't have to sit here and listen to this shit. You have violated and disrespected me for the last time; once again you are in pure violation—*out of order, I'm done!"*

I grab my pillow and storm out of the room, hoping he won't follow me, but he does and continues to go on and on with all this unnecessary yelling and screaming.

In my mind I'm saying, *Damn, you go, girl, you got his ass. You flipped the script on that ass tonight. Ding, ding, ding, another knockout, man down, win once again. Good job, E!*

I'm not even hearing him right now, so he's doing all that yelling and screaming for nothing!

You see, men tend to think it's all about them, but I'm that chick, who will show and tell different. Most men like Malik have good intentions to be good men, but typically what happens is that their little-boy tendencies override their ability to be that good man, because they stop thinking with their brain, and start thinking with their penis, and that's where the problems come in. For instance, like not knowing when you need to bring your ass home. Come on now, as a grown man with a wife and kids, it's some things you just don't do, and that is one of them.

Over the years, while dealing with Malik, and all his shit; I've learned that, as a woman you have to be able to have control; sometimes that means sitting back and not using up all your good ammunition until times like this. I like to call it the sex switch and spin. That's when you think like the opposite sex and turn the situation around to fit your needs.

Instead of you yelling and screaming like most women do, let him do it all. Leave him confused, and you just relax and bring up something he did that was very hurtful to you. I don't care if it was twenty years ago. If you remember what happened twenty years ago, bring it up. Then while he's yelling and screaming and talking shit, you're not even tripping because it's going in one ear and out the other. You're just waiting until it's your turn to talk so you can blast his ass by bringing up old random shit that he did wrong, to you in the relationship; whether it was a day ago or twenty years ago. It all works the same; leaving him feeling emotionally dysfunctional and guilty.

Right now Malik is going crazy, yelling, screaming, and stomping around; once again, his little-boy tendencies have kicked in and he can't control them. But I know what he's thinking. He's thinking that by doing all this acting out, that he is going to break me down and make me lose control of the situation, possibly even scare me into doing what he wants me to do. But what he doesn't realize is that I've been one step ahead of him since I walked in the door: and about me losing control? *It won't happen! It's not an option! I've already won!*

I've already Sex Switched and Spun his ass, and he don't even have a clue what's about to happen next. He's just wasting my time and his energy with all this yelling and screaming; the game was over before it started. *See, men don't know about the infamous power of the black woman for real. We can be just as vindictive as a man, but the difference between men and women is that women know what we're doing, and we move with caution and wisdom. Men just make moves and do and say anything without thinking first. We don't. It's always our choice, and we always have a plan and a point to our vindication.*

I'm tired and ready to go to bed; plus, the day I had with Drake today has me on cloud nine, so I wish Malik's ass would shut up and just let it go and go to bed and let me sleep on the couch. I just want to say, "Shut the fuck up. I can't fuck you tonight because I've already fucked Drake earlier today!" But I have to stay on my square, and besides, that might get my ass *Snapped* on and dead, for real. LOL. I can't let vindication override what's important. I will not let Malik's negative verbiage and body language get to me. As he keeps pointing in my face talking shit, I just keep tuning him out. I will not lose my state of being over words and emotions, because he still hasn't realized that he has lost...

Malik can yell and scream all night, saying shit he will regret tomorrow, if not by the end of the night. Because just like tonight he wants some ass and ain't gone get it. Tomorrow will be the same thing, if he keeps on going. And one thing about the wifey's ass: out of all the asses in the world, there's no other ass like it, especially when they really want wifey's. Oh! But if he does decide to go and play with those tramps that keep him out all night, and get some ass from them: good. That's cool too, because he would only be doing me a favor, by helping me save all my energy for the Man in the Hat (Drake) for our next encounter.

I'm a woman. If I can get away with all the stuff I pull off with Drake. I know damn well a group of guys don't have Malik's ass out all night—at least not every night anyway. And if I thought that was the case, I would be playing myself. I'm not stupid. I'm just passive because I want to be. I just sit back and don't say anything unless it's times like this, because I have my own indiscretion to deal with.

I plop down on the couch, face full of anger, only to hear Malik's ass right behind me. Instead of yelling he is just calling my name now, continuously, like a child saying, "Mama" over and over again. *Damn,* I think to myself.

"What!" I yell.

Malik just stands there for a minute hovering over me, looking big and stupid. He finally says in a soft whisper, "Baby, baby!" But I won't answer; I have to act it out to the fullest. "Baby," he says again. "I'm sorry. I wasn't calling you a bitch, I was just saying it like, you know, you're my bitch. You know, like my boo, my shorty, my lady.

"Man E, you made me mad; you're always bringing up some other woman, bitch shit, like I'm sneaking around on you or something. Like I got time to waste, playing with these bitches out here, all day and night. Like that's all my life consists of, is drinking and playing with bitches.

"I'm a hustler; I work a nine to five, but when I'm done with that, I'm trying to work another one in the streets for you and my family. And sometimes that means hanging out with people when I really don't want to, but I just do it for connection and marketing purposes. I'm a real estate investor. I can't get where I need to be if I don't meet and network with new people. I love you, and I don't want to be with anyone else but you. You're my support system. You're all I need.

"Those few years when we were apart, I thought I was going to lose my mind, along with my money. Just me thinking about you and my kids being around some other man was going to drive me crazy, and I knew you and your attorneys—your buddy Larry and all his connections; especially that wife of his, whatever her name is—were going to take me to the bank. Just joking about the bank, E, but I'm dead serious about loving you and those kids and never wanting to be in that position of not knowing again. You know I was out drinking at Club 906, with the guys last night. I called and texted you all night. You know how it is when we all get together. Baby, I do not be on any bullshit. I was just out kicking it and mingling and lost track of time. It won't happen again. I promise.

"You never say anything about it any other time, so I just assumed you trusted me and understood that the past was the past. I thought you had reestablished trust in me again, as your husband who loves you more than you know. I'm sorry! Please come back to bed, don't act like this. It's late and we both have to get up early in the morning. This is crazy, or as you would say, bananas...This whole thing is just crazy and stupid. Come on; you know this isn't for us anymore. I've been really trying. I don't want to go back down that road with you ever again."

*Man, he almost has me; he always did have the gift of gab. I feel bad and I'm starting to get a little weak in the knees. This is a switch for me. Man, he is very convincing and really seems sincere, but I still have to stick it out and stick to my guns on this one.*

"Malik, you do and say this all the time. You know why I don't say anything anymore, because I'm tired. I'm tired of your late nights and partying, because yes, it's still considered a party if you're at a bar. Whether you're marketing, mingling, networking, or knitting, you're at a bar drinking and hanging out. You need to get it together and act like a husband and not like a twenty-three-year-old frat boy. You're not twenty-three years old anymore. Grow up!"

"OK, OK, OK, Eva. I'm sorry; no more staying out after midnight. Regardless of what's going on, I'm coming home. I don't want to fight and argue about this no more. Now would you please come back to bed, before the kids wake up? I was just tripping. I've had a stressful day today. I have a lot of pressure on me; things that I don't even mention to you. This business has me stressed E, but I'm sorry. I don't know what I was thinking, calling you out of your name, regardless of how I thought I was portraying it. That was totally uncalled for and immature of me. You did not deserve all that yelling and screaming I was doing either. Again, I apologize, E, I just love you so much, that's all, and sometimes my mind wanders, which leads to a reaction like this."

I looked up at him. "You know what, Malik? I've had a long, stressful day at the office today too. I'm PMSin' like crazy, constipated, and not only that, but I'm tired as H.E. double hockey sticks—so tired that I didn't even take a bath tonight, so stressed out at work that I had to go to the mall and buy a pair of shoes just to clear my mind.

"Yet I did not bring my stress home with me like you did. I brought home smiles, hugs, and kisses, along with food to ensure that my family was comfortable and had a decent meal on the dinner table, and this was the thanks I got. Not 'how was your day, honey,' or 'thanks for the food, honey; you even got my favorite Chinese food, honey.' All I've gotten from you today is negativity and more stress. I heard it all up in your voice earlier when I spoke with you on the phone after leaving the mall. I knew it was going to be an issue about something tonight. I could feel it in my spirit.

"I'm tired of every time I'm not on your schedule for having sex, it's a problem. This has got to stop, Malik, and yeah, you should be sorry, because I don't deserve to be treated like this; I've never deserved it. And the next time you even think about calling me a bitch in any shape, form, or fashion, that's going to be your ass, mister. I'm going to let you slide this one time and blame it on your stressful day, because I share your pain today, but next time don't come home taking your stressful days out on me. I'm your wife, not your bitch! I'm the one who is supposed to turn your stressful day into a good night. But I can't do that if you're walking around with a chip on your shoulder because I stopped by the mall or just don't feel like stroking yo penis."

I grab my pillow off the couch with that same little mischievous grin from earlier, only this time smiling on the inside, and head back into the bedroom, thinking in the back of my mind. *Girl, you are ruthless. You tore his ass up tonight, and you the one been cheating! And yeah, he may be all apologetic but he still ain't getting any. I hope he knows that before I get into this bed.*

But by now, between all the fussing and fighting, he's drained anyway. I can tell by the way he just gets in the bed, still in his robe. He is too drained to even think about sex, because he never falls asleep in his robe; he's just happy I came back to bed and that I'm done fussing about that word *bitch*.

When I get in the bed, he scoots over and cuddles me to his body, holding me as close as he possibly can and squeezes me tight, then says, "I love you E, I love you more than you know. I know I've made a lot of mistakes in this marriage, but I promise I'm going to get it right this time." He kisses me on the back of my neck and then drifts off to sleep like a two-year-old little boy.

Me, on the other hand, I'm wide-awake. I'm just lying there, thinking. Thinking about everything that has transpired tonight and how it is all a reflection of me this time, and the feelings I have for another man and what, if anything, will be the outcome of this whole situation. And you know what I had to ask myself. *I have been called a bitch, lost a few hours of sleep, and had a terrible argument with my husband because of my sneaky secretes, and is it all worth it?*

And after asking myself that question, the first thought that comes to my mind is, an E, thought, and her answer was, *Yes sir! And I will probably do it all over again next week.*

Then, in the back of my mind—I'm talking far back—I hear Eva say, *that's messed up; you are the one who needs to get it together and act like a wife this time.* Of course I ignore Eva's thoughts and override them with the thoughts of E.

*Shit, I'm sure Malik has done it to me a thousand times before and probably still is, and I don't know how he thinks that this little show he put on tonight, acting like he's the perfect husband, is going to excuse his little midnight missing escapades. But it's cool because I know the truth and right now our relationship is fragile and hanging on by a thread. So whatever works for the moment is good for me, just as long as it doesn't interfere with me and the Man in the Hat!*

# 5

## Sun of a Reality

*I* can hear Malik in the bathroom taking a shower. I roll over and take a look at the clock and notice that it's eight in the morning. Normally Malik leaves out with the kids, at around seven, so it's unusual for him to be just now taking a shower. I guess after our little escapade last night, he overslept or is just tired, like I am. I would like to get up and possibly get a light workout in before I start my day, but since I'm feeling a little guilty about yesterday and last night, I'll just lay here and play sleep until Malik leaves for work. Then I'll get up.

It's always like this the day after. Right when the sunlight hits your face, you know that it's back to reality and back to the same old routine. You lie in bed trying to piece it all together, thinking about the whole scenario of the situation, as it replays back and forth in your mind, asking yourself was it really worth it. See, yesterday, I was caught up on my emotions and so filled up with Drake's love potion that anything and everything was all good. But today, oh today, it's a tad bit different.

I lie in bed thinking about last night and the horrible fight Malik and I had, along with the lies I told and the wicked Angela Bassett performance I put on. (That, if I must say, was an Oscar-winning performance). I also think about those shoes I bought that I didn't need, and how they were a waste of time and money, and have to go back. Then I think about the kids. I hope they slept straight through it all, this time and didn't hear any of what was going on.

I know that because of me and my indiscretions; Malik's day has been thrown off as well as mine. On top of all that, I'm so tired and drained, I don't even feel like getting out of the bed to go into the office; my body is tired and my mind is mentally drained from all the deceitful thoughts and concocted stories I had to make up. Then, to top it off, for the next few days or so, I'm going to be under surveillance, watched like a hawk by Malik. Therefore, I'll be walking around on eggshells, being cautious not to slip up and say or do anything that might incriminate me. And heaven forbid, I have to actually go to the mall. I can hear Malik now: *I thought you said you went to the mall on Thursday; that was a bunch of bull. You're always talking about me being on BS, you be on BS all the time. All you do is lie yourself.* I know Malik like a book. He is going to hold on to everything that was said yesterday, in that little pea-size brain of his; he'll sit back and try to catch me tripping. But guess what, Malik? *It won't happen,* just like it didn't happen last night.

Malik always takes a shower and gets dressed in the guest bedroom when I'm still in the bed so he doesn't disturb me, so I don't know if he's about to leave or if he is still getting dressed or what's going on, and it's driving me bananas. All I know is that I don't hear the shower anymore. I do know that I cannot keep lying here too much longer, faking sleep; I have got to get up, and get my day started.

I finally hear the garage door going down, which means he's leaving.

"Thank God!" I scream and jump up from under the covers. "Man, I could not pretend sleep too much longer."

I jump up out of the bed, run to the window, and peep out to make sure he's gone. Sure enough, his car is heading out the subdivision. Eagerly, I reach to turn on my lamp so that I can look under the bed and get my cell phone, where I always hide it; in its favorite spot, in one of my house shoes, set on silent mood. I notice a sticky note on my lamp that says, "I Love You, E! Have a Good Day, Call Me When You Get To Work, Didn't Want To Wake You, Love, Malik!"

I just smile and say, "Awwww, he is really over-the-top this time." A second of guilt enters my spirit about what I had done yesterday, and then it's gone a second later, and I find myself eagerly on my knees, feeling around for the house shoe I had placed my cell phone in.

You see, I have to hide my phone because Malik is a cell phone snatcher. He lurks during the night, when I'm asleep. He preys on cell phones that are left unattended, mine especially, and once found, it becomes an open book. He likes to scroll through the calls looking for clues, as if I'm stupid enough to have any number left on there that would be detrimental to my health anyway. Oh, and God forbid I have it locked; he will go crazy and start screaming like a madman, just like he was doing last night! *"What married woman locks her phone? Where they do that at?"*

On and on and on he will go, with all the reasons why a married woman, should not have to lock her phone and all the negative reasons, why a married woman would lock her phone. So to prevent his emotional phone-locking breakdown and me getting caught up in it, I just keep it out of sight. Out of sight, out of mind!

Plus, come on now. I'm much smarter than the average cheating wife. I'm a married, cheating genius— if you ask me. Men do stupid stuff, and forgetful things, like leaving their phone laying around, unlocked with all the numbers of the chicks that they're cheating with in the phone, listed under names like QT, Kool, Cali, Juicy—stupid names that bring attention to themselves, when we phone scroll stalking, *'cause you done got in the shower and left your phone on the table, unlocked and it's going off and now I'm going through it. LOL!*

Malik has done it more than once, and has gotten caught up more than once, because of it. I just figured; he must have wanted me to go through it because if he didn't, he would have hid it under the bed, in his house shoe, on silent mood like I do. Men are just dumb and irresponsible, when it comes to being sneaky and cheating anyway.

But not women, especially those who have something to hide, like me. I make sure all my T's are crossed and all my I's are dotted, even before I pull into the driveway. Then I do a double-check right before walking into the house just to be certain that everything's straight. The funny thing about Malik's phone-snatching ass is that he doesn't know, that I know, he be doing it. Sometimes I will just leave my phone sitting around on purpose, so when he's done scrolling through it, checking all the numbers and all the text messages: incoming and outgoing, and come up empty-handed and clueless, he feels stupid and embarrassed. Yet it makes him feel a little more secure and relieved with me, so it works for me too. See, I told you; I'm always two steps ahead, smarter than the average cheating wife and unlike Malik, smarter than a fifth grader.

I scroll through my cell phone, trying to see if Drake has called or left me a text message, but he hasn't. I'm a little disappointed, but I'll give him a pass this time, since he did such a marvelous job on Lady Blues yesterday. I can't believe I'm still living off those memories this morning; I'm having shooting orgasms just thinking about it. *Damn!* What a man, what a man, what a mighty good man. "Yes, he is," I sing in my Salt-N-Pepa voice while shaking my head from side to side in disbelief. I guess the slightest thought of Drake makes that small feeling of regret and guilt fade away, huh?

I check to see if my girl Nyla has called. This is the best part of the day after, once you've gotten past the guilt. This is the part when you call your girl and tell her all about your little rendezvous, every little freaky, nasty, scandalous detail of your little sexcapade. Then, after you're done with the good stuff, you can tell her about the fight you had with your husband and how you swindled your way out of it again—the entire highlights and even the lowlights. It's like an instant replay, all in fun and laughter, though.

But, first things first; before I can call Nyla, I have something very important I must do, and that is take a bath. Oh my God! Try going to bed after being tossed around like a salad, lifted up and over, spun down and back around again, like a roller-coaster ride, then smothered in love potion mixed with sweat. You can't even imagine. It's OK when you just had sex with your husband and fall asleep sticky, but to fall asleep sticky in bed with your husband, with another man's stickiness all over you—well, that's just a nasty combination and a little trifling if you ask me. But I guess God had to make me pay some kind of way for my infidelity. This is probably how I'm appearing to him spiritually anyway right now. *TRIFLING!*

Laura Mercier is calling my name; I soak in the tub for an hour, lying there just reminiscing about Drake. This man is like hypnotic. The thought of him lingers in my head like my name. It's crazy. Sometimes I honestly think I'm losing focus on what's really important, which is my children, my marriage—the platform that we are now on; even though the foundation underneath, is raggedy as hell, it's still what we've built together.

*What will be the outcome of all this? What exactly will it be? I don't want to leave this lifestyle that I've become so accustom to, but I don't want to leave Drake either.*

Drake and I were not supposed to fall in love. This was only supposed to be a short but sweet play thing—nothing serious—something more similar to a one-night stand. I honestly have love for my husband; I do, even with all his faults. Malik is still my husband and a good father, especially when it comes to providing for his family. He is naturally a provider and I know he loves us, even with all his issues and his drunken disease (what he likes to call it). His whole focus on life has been making sure that his family is financially stable and secure, and so far he's done a good job with that.

I can remember that on our fifth wedding anniversary, he bought me a black Porsche Cayenne Turbo. He's always showering me with gifts—everything from $2,000 Chloe handbags to $7,000 Cartier watches. Malik and I have been married for over eleven years now. We were together three years prior to getting married. During our time together we've had two lovely children: Camilla, our daughter, who is thirteen, and Cameron, our son, who is eleven.

With his real estate investment firm and my CPA firm, Malik and I are doing very well for ourselves and our family; together we have established a rather secure and stable financial platform. Basically, we're practically living every married couple's dream—two lovely children, great careers, a lovely home, and the perfect marriage on paper. At least that's how it appears.

When I met Malik, I was fresh out of high school, and he was in college finishing up his second degree and already making major cash in real estate; I thought he was the best thing that had ever happened to me. Right from the start he was the perfect gentleman: tall and handsome, intelligent, very neat, and he always smelled good.

The scent of his Fahrenheit used to drive me wild. We would travel all the time, going everywhere the elite crowd was going. The fights in Vegas, South Beach in the spring, Atlanta Freaknik; he even took me on a trip to Cancun with him and all his friends. I would hear his frat brothers talking in the background.

"Malik, man, why would you bring sand to the beach?"

Malik would just laugh at them and say, "Man, that's my lady, and I love my sand. Don't be mad at me because I got me a young, untouched tenderoni and y'all messing with all those tainted old tramps."

Malik has always been the outgoing party type of guy, and I would always be right there, by his side. I was his lady and I was going anywhere he was going. It was all about me, and as long as I was happy, he was happy.

See, because Malik was older and more experienced than I was, he made me feel secure and comfortable. He had already accomplished everything I was trying to achieve: the education, the money, the house, the car. He was already set and I was still living at home with my mother trying to figure it out. So, I felt like Malik was the answer to everything I needed to figure out.

I would spend weeks at a time at his house. I would go over there planning to spend one night, only to stay for weeks.

"I don't want you to leave, not even to go home and get clothes," Malik would say. "I'll just go out and buy you some new ones." He would buy me shoes, clothes, lingerie, cosmetics, and anything else I needed, all because he didn't want me to go home. I guess because I'd never had a man in my life growing up and was raised by a single mother, I was overwhelmed and excited. I had never experienced a man who was so giving and so caring—a man had never showed me all this attention Malik was showing me. Malik made me feel special and loved. There was nothing I wanted that I could not have with Malik.

I had grown up as the youngest child in a single-parent home, with two sister and three brothers. Struggling in the Peabody's of downtown St. Louis, so I had never experienced having anything and everything I wanted at my fingertips. But with Malik I didn't even have to ask. I loved me some Malik Ewing; he had swept me right off my feet. My nose was wide open and so were my legs'—which is how I got pregnant with Camilla. I had never felt love like this before, or at least what I thought resembled love. There were no limits to what this man would do for me. He was my man, and I was a kid in love. You couldn't tell me anything.

And now the same thing applies to our children: there are no limits when it comes to them. Malik and I together give them anything their little heart's desire; which is everything, I never had as a child and more.

Any woman would love to be in my shoes and in my bed; even with all Malik's drama, and yet I'm running around hopping in somebody else's. *What is wrong with me?*

Besides Malik spoiling me with extraordinary gifts and cars, believe it or not, he and I still have fun together, when we're feeling each other. But when we are not, it's crazy. It's like a seesaw relationship with us. One minute we're stepping out on the town together and screwing on the balcony; the next day we're stepping out on each other and ready to throw each other over the balcony, and it's gotten worse since I've met Drake.

Our marriage has been on the rocks for years now, even before Drake entered the picture. I thought it would be better when I moved back home, but nothing has changed. It was better for the first few months, now it's right back to what made me leave him in the first place. It's right back to the same old scene, with Malik hanging out all night, coming home after hours, and constantly getting drunk all the time. Because of that alone, Malik and I have had our fair share of problems, which has caused us to separate on more than one occasion. I guess this last separation was the separation of all separations. This one was the worst of the worst; because this time I brought back poison to our marriage, and unlike Malik's poison, his name is not Jack Daniels. It's Drake Grimley.

My love and devotion for another man is the poison that has infected our marriage even more. I know it; I can feel the venom burning inside my heart and soul, I can smell the scent of it burning in the atmosphere of our home, and all over my body.

But, I still yearn for this poison every day, though. Knowing it has infected my well-being and created an unhealthy lifestyle, not only for my marriage, but also for my inner person. Not to mention what it has done with my relationship with God—heck, my best friend's husband is a minister, and I haven't been to church in months. Too busy trying to have silent moments with Drake. It's a shame before God; how I've been running around, acting like and adulterous whore; I know better.

My mother is probably turning over in her grave. Even though our family was dysfunctional growing up, my mother still made us go to church, and taught us to respect the Word of God. So I got the Word of the Lord down in me. But just like the rest of my siblings, after mom passed, I fell off the God wagon and into the hands of the enemy too.

One of my sisters got hooked on drugs. The other one has four kids, three baby-daddies, and ain't *ever* been married, to either one of them. One of my brothers is confused about his sexuality— currently going through the transformation to become a woman; done changed his name from, Reginald to Regina. *Where they do that at?* My brother Roger is doing time in jail, for selling drugs; which is what caused my sister Raven to get hooked on drugs: helping him sell them. My youngest brother, Ronnie is the only sibling I have; that I feel is actually doing something positive with his life. Ronnie lives in Los Angeles; he's married, doesn't have any kids and owns his own fitness business. Then there's me— the adulterous, perfect-on-paper, married, whore.

Infidelity is ruining my life, and my marriage, one day at a time and now it's burning from both ends. I can't even be intimate with my husband the way a wife should be anymore, because my body doesn't feel unless it's with Drake; my body shifts into numb gear at the site of my husband, rejecting his passion and cringing at his touch like a reflex. That's when you know the vibe that used to be has lost its rhythm and is no longer there, and that's because it lies with someone else. *Drake!*

This is really the reason why there's so much friction between Malik and me; I know it is. It's not about him staying out late, getting drunk, and seeing other women, because he has been doing that for years, and I still stood by, supporting him as my husband, being devoted to the life that we built together and this family. But now, it's on me. I've changed. I've let someone else in, and I've vacated my position of being a wife to my husband. So it's about the void that I bring to our home now. And Malik recognizes it, this is what rubs Malik the wrong way and causes him to question our relationship, because he doesn't understand the situation and the reason for my disconnection and/or my standoffish actions. *I'm sure.*

All he can see is rejection. All he can feel is isolation. The love and romance that used to belong to my husband, regardless of what he has done, now belongs to Drake. The passionate moments that Malik and I used to share have been cursed by indiscretion and infidelity, now on both of our behalf.

No longer is the blood only on his hands; it's now on mine as well. Our marriage is lost—lost in complications and confusion. The hindrance of distrust and dishonesty between the two of us is spreading like a virus. Sometimes I think, this could be the reason why Malik does stay out all night, drinking and hanging out. He's afraid and fearful that his wife has stopped making deposits to the love bank, and our marriage is about to go bankrupt. To be honest, I don't see a way for us to fix this, unless I call it off with Drake. Even then, I still don't think it would work because I don't think I will ever trust Malik or be *in love* with him again. If this thing is going to work and I'm going to be delivered from this bondage, God is going to have to step in and take the wheel.

I sometimes wonder why I even came back. Then I think about Camilla and Cameron and ask myself, "If it wasn't for my children, where would I be?" Then I answer back and say, "Where my heart really resides and my future waits, and that is with Drake!"

I would never want to make my children the strings that are holding my marriage together, because in reality they are old enough to understand what's going on, and they pretty much know that their father and I have been going through a lot over the years. They've seen us separate all those times, witnessed all the fussing and fighting that constantly goes on between us, so I know they really know it's not all good with us. They just have so much respect for both of us and our marriage; they would never say anything, so they go on acting like it's all good, as if they are just as happy as I pretend to be. So just like them, I continue to pretend because their happiness is my happiness. They deserve to live a happy life with both parents, stress free. I want them to be able to proudly say they live in a two-parent household, with their biological parents, like I wished for when I was a child.

That said; I can't let them down.

As a parent there sometimes comes a time when you have to put your happiness on hold in order to secure and ensure that your children's happiness is being fulfilled. After all, they didn't ask to be here. I feel like I owe them at least that, which is why I made the decision to move back home this last time and every time before when Malik and I had separated. Whether it was my decision or his, we would decide to pull it together, come together, and make it work for our kids and for our vision for this family.

They deserve a nice home and a complete family. All kids do. They don't deserve to grow up like I did, in a broken home without a relationship with their father. So in saying all that, I'm very adamant about making sure my lovely children grow up in a normal and stable home, with both their mother and their father.

I don't want them to end up like I did, searching and looking for love because you never really got it at home, so that when the first person comes along and shows any sign of love, you latch on, not even getting a chance to live your own life or discover who you really are. That is what leaves me stuck in a marriage that I'm unhappy in, stealing silent moments with Drake and yearning for the day I can say, "Honey, I'm home!" and meet him at the front door, instead of Malik.

*These are the heart-wrenching dreams I have to hold on to for about six or seven more years, till the kids are grown and gone.*

"It's either dream like this and continue living inside this love triangle, or let Drake go and work on my marriage with my husband, a marriage that I know will never work." I say out loud.

After that, I just look up to the ceiling and ask God, *Why am I doing this? What have I gotten myself into and how can I fix it?* Tears begin to roll down my face as I cry out for answers. *How can my marriage be fixed, when as soon as I wake up in the morning and the sunlight hits my face, my stomach start turning because of the yearning and hunger I feel inside for another man? How can it be fixed when every minute of my day is spent thinking about Drake and our silent moments together, and how long will it be before I can steal another one? How can I focus on what should be the most important things in my life when the only thing on my mind is another man and how good I feel when I'm with him?*

The love I have for Drake is ruining everything. It's not that I'm losing focus on what's important; it's that I'm focused on following my heart, and my heart leads me right to Drake, so that surpasses everything else. I love this man—truly I do. How did I let it get this far? I don't know.

This man has come into my life and made me weak yet whole. When I was lost, broken, and going through, he was the one comforting me. He made me feel like a brand-new woman, a new and improved woman, a woman of substance, who does not need validation through monetary or tangible things, a woman who knows how to feel genuine love and also how to give it—and not just because of what he can do for me or give me, but because I enjoy doing for him, and giving to him.

The connections we share are all natural and effortless; the chemistry we have is magical. When both of our hearts are beating in rhythm as one, while making love, and every breath I take he breathes in after me, assures me that this sign could only be a sign of true love.

He is my Mr. Hold My Hand, Love Me Right, and Relax My Mind, all in one. He is a reflection of me and the image of my heart. I chase his style and crave his charm, only to get it for a few hours a week. He eats away at me like heroin. I'm sick when I can't have him. This is how I know that this is love, not because of a purse, a watch or a new car, but because I'm content with just him.

And yes, Drake may be my other life, but he is the only man who holds the other pieces to the rest of my life. When I look for me—when I forget who I am—I can always find myself when I'm with him, because he makes me whole all over again. He is... my new normal!

# 6

## BFF, You Home-Wrecking Husband Thief

"Hey, Ny! This is Eva. Call me when you get this message. I'm on my way into the office; I'm planning on taking a half day. I was hoping we could do lunch, my treat. Oh! And, yeah, I forgot. I was with you-know-who yesterday, so you know I have an earful waiting for you; that I'm sure your church-girl ears aren't going to want to hear, but I'm going to tell you anyway, like always. Ooh! *That man.* Girl, I get wet just thinking about him. Call me, love you, bye!"

Nyla aka Ny is my girl and the godmother of my son, Cameron. She's like a sister to me, the smart one I never had, because both of my sisters turned out to be Project Rejects. Don't get me wrong, I love both of my biological sisters, but they both have issues, and the biggest issue of all is that they're both stupid. But Nyla, I love her to death; I don't know what I would do without her. She's the spare part to my brain, when mine is either broke down or just having technical difficulties and can't seem to get it all together.

All I have to do is call on Nyla, and she will put everything back into perspective for me. What I want to hear, what I don't want to hear, or what I need to hear—whatever the situation may call for—she will lay it all out, firm, clear, and straight to the point, whether I like it or not. Her motto is: *even if you can't stand the truth, you still have to deal with the truth, so deal with it and get over it!*

I've known Nyla for about eleven years now; I met her right before, Cameron was born. Nyla just happens to be the wife of Malik's good friend, Jamal. I was introduced to Nyla at a cookout Malik and I gave a few years back, or should I say a very long time ago. It's rather funny the way we met, when I go back and think about it, because before Nyla and I became friends, I didn't like her. I used to call her Nyla the Annihilator. Jamal had just gone through a vicious breakup with his ex-fiancée, Paris. Paris was never a close friend of mine, but we would talk and hang out occasionally on the strength of Malik and Jamal; I pretty much knew everything that was going on in their household pertaining to Jamal and Paris's relationship and all the drama involved.

I knew that Jamal had been taking Paris through a lot of trials and tribulations as far as their relationship was concerned and that Jamal had been lying and staying out all night, coming home drunk, and going out of town every weekend, saying it was work related, when really it wasn't. He wasn't spending any time with Paris or their two boys, just acting a fool, if you ask me—kind of like what Malik's been doing. I tell you; that cheating spirit must have jumped off Jamal and onto Malik, but anyway...

I found out later that the reason Jamal was acting like a complete fool was because he was a fool—a fool in love with another woman (Nyla) and creeping out on Paris. I can recall Paris calling Malik's house on numerous occasions—interrupting our pillow-talking time with nonsense—asking me if Malik was there. Once I put Malik on the phone, she would question him about Jamal and his whereabouts. *As if!*

I can still hear her now. "Malik, have you seen Jamal? Do you know where he might be? Can you call him and tell him to call home? Malik, you don't think anything has happened to him, do you? I hope he is all right. I've been calling him and it's going straight to his voice mail; I haven't heard from him all day, and I'm getting worried, and it's getting late. If he calls you, have him to call me. I'll keep texting him."

All that old crazy BS. I would look at Malik while he would be looking stupid and dumb on that phone, answering all those questions with all those *no* answers, and saying, "Couldn't be me! I wish you would!" I mean, I would get an attitude like Jamal was my fiancé. Malik would just tell me to be quiet, go to sleep, and stay out of other people's affairs. I wanted so bad to say, "Yeah, it's an affair all right and if you don't want me in it, then you need to tell her crybaby, whining ass to stop calling here, interrupting our PT, and then I wouldn't be in it. If it was you, you already know I wouldn't be calling looking for you. I would be hiding outside our house behind the bushes with my stupid stick, waiting on your black behind to walk up so I could beat the hell out of you with it. I surely wouldn't be calling your boy's house in the middle of the night disturbing his groove, crying, asking questions that I know I'm not going to get a correct answer to.

Next time she calls, Malik, why don't you just tell her the truth: 'Yeah, Jamal, all right, yeah. He's good, oh, and by the way, the only thing that has happened to him is that he took another route before coming home, called *the road to another woman's house*.' Malik would just look at me, shake his head, and say "Girl you crazy!"

See, this is the reason why I didn't really care for Nyla, because although I didn't have official evidence that Jamal was creeping around with Nyla during the times Paris would call looking for him, it didn't matter. I had woman's intuition, and that's more potent than evidence.

So from that particular night, just like all the other nights when Paris would be calling, and looking for Jamal, it stuck in my head like a piece of gum that these were the signs of a cheating man and that Jamal was that man. I didn't know with whom, he was cheating with at the time, but I knew Jamal was cheating, and I took it personal. So when the cat finally came out the bag about Nyla and Jamal, I started to have flashbacks of all those nights Paris was calling and crying to Malik. I put two and two together, that Nyla was the home-wrecking husband thief and Jamal had been cheating with her all that time.

See, after Nyla came in the picture, Paris didn't have a chance; all she had was a dream, a ring, and a wedding dress that never got worn! I was so mad, that you would have thought Paris and I were cool, but it wasn't even about Paris any more. It was about men trying to be slick and getting away with it; with women like Nyla, who come in and infiltrate other women's territories.

See, what men don't understand is that women never forget anything. We are like sponges; we absorb and store. It could have been something that happened with a girl in grade school, and we will remember her name, what she had on that day, and what period it was, when whatever went down, went down. And if we happen to stumble upon a Tic Tac of a hint, we will put the pieces of the puzzle together like we work for *Cold Case*. Don't ever get it twisted.

So, this incident alone, which had nothing to do with me, is why I could not stand Mrs. Nyla. Although Paris and I weren't the best of friends, and I thought she acted a little slow when it came to men and being aware of infiltrator's like Nyla, I was still a woman and a fiancée too, and I couldn't imagine what she must have been going through—all those nights: all that hurt and pain she must have been feeling.

What if that was Malik, and I was wearing Paris's shoes? You can never be too sure in relationships, because it could happen to you, and then how would you handle the situation? I always told myself as a young girl, because of the way my dad left my mother, that if I ever got married, I would never, ever give a man too much glory, because if and when he let me down, who would be there to pick me up? I'll be crazy and crying myself into a depression, and he'll be OK because he will have someone like Nyla, who thinks it's OK to mess up happy homes in order to make theirs better, and I would be left to clothe and feed my kids just like my mama was.

To me Nyla was like scum, gum on the bottom of my shoe, a foot rash that itched like hell and wouldn't leave. After seeing all the drama Paris went through with Jamal, it left a very bad taste in my mouth about Nyla and what she did. As a woman, I wanted to seek revenge for Paris.

So, when Malik mentioned to me that Jamal would be bringing Nyla to a cookout we were having a year or so after all this transpired, I flipped my lid. I was now the wife and I told him that I didn't want any home-wrecking whore around me or my husband. I told Malik I just couldn't believe Jamal after everything he and Paris had built together. How could he just leave her and the boys like he did and just move on with his life as if nothing ever happened—as if Paris was never his high school sweet-heart, college sweetheart, baby mama, and fiancée? He didn't care about how it made her feel or look. And what about their neighbors, their co-workers, the teachers at the school: what were they thinking?

See, Jamal and Paris graduated and worked at the same college (Wash U) together; he was a professor, and she worked in administration. Their home was right on the campus, basically campus living, so all the stu-dents and all the employees technically lived in that same area. I mean, damn, how would Paris bounce back from that? It was just all too unclear to me, and I was completely outdone. How could he just drop and leave everything he worked so hard to build for a woman he really knew noth-ing about? That didn't make any sense to me.

Besides, all I knew about Nyla was that she was a home wrecker. As far as I knew, she could have been plotting to hook up one of her home-wrecking ho friends with Malik. You know how women do. You know the ones with no morals or respect for the wife or themselves. My whole thought about the situation was not that Paris was my friend, but that I may have only been a newlywed, but I was still a wife and a woman first. And now that I had finally made it to wifey status, I'd be darn if some husband-hunting, scandalous home intruder like Nyla was going to come in and infiltrate my home.

So, as I was just standing in the backyard, sipping on a glass of Manajatwa red wine, laughing at Malik from a distance, over there in front of the grill, flipping steaks and trying to eat a hotdog all at the same time. Looking stupid with this apron on that read, "Kiss the Cook," along with the matching chef hat; like he was throwing down. All of a sudden this pearl-white convertible Mercedes E350 pulls in the driveway.

"Who the hell!" I yelled, and it was like everybody stopped drinking and eating mid-laugh and yelled, "That look like Jamal! And is that Tyra Banks?" I had to put down my glass of wine, because I had already been trying to quit drinking, but now I knew it was really time, 'cause apparently, I had had one too many.

Jamal got out of the car and yelled, "Hey, E! What's up? Where's Malik? I have someone I want y'all to meet!"

Now, we had not seen Jamal in over a year since the separation drama and all that mess with Paris went down, so I was really surprised at the way he was acting—all happy and excited to see us.

I could not believe my eyes; who was this man yelling at me? Was this Jamal, Malik's friend, Paris's ex-fiancé; this man was a fancier version of the Jamal I knew, he looked like his name could have been (Jamal-ja) like Target is called (Tar-ja). I could not believe what I was seeing. I know a lot can happen in a year, but dang, Jamal was a different person. He had turned into an upgraded, excited, metrosexual sex symbol.

By now Malik had abandoned the grill and walked up to me to see what all the fuss was about. As Jamal walked around to the other side of the car and opened the driver's door for who I thought looked like Tyra Banks, I whispered to Malik, "I've never seen him do that before."

He grabbed her by the hand and walked over to Malik and me and says, "Nyla, these are my good friends, Eva and Malik. Malik and Eva, this is Nyla." If you could have seen the look on his face and the way his eyes lit up when he said, "This is Nyla," you would have thought he was a kid at Christmas, and this was his gift from heaven. He looked at her as if she were an angel who had just flown down from heaven to take him home.

As they stood in front of me, I could not help but notice the loving energy and the vibe they had between each other; it was overwhelming and breathtaking, like something out of a romance movie. The trees were blowing, the birds were chirping, and the sun had a rainbow behind it. I had never seen Jamal like this before. Not only was his demeanor different, but so was his appearance. He was a changed man. This was not the boring, self-absorbed, no-name jeans, Reebok tennis shoes, fleece zip-up-wearing man I used to know. The man standing before me was hip, full of life and happy energy. *Wow, is this what a year of good lovin' can do for you!* I thought. Jamal had on Prada tennis shoes, True Religion jeans, and a snug V-neck T-shirt that read UNPREDICTABLE backward (ELBATICIDERPNU) that showed off his new muscular body. What the hell was going on? The T-shirt alone was enough for me. Malik and I stood there looking in awe. Then I looked over at Nyla, and that's when it all came to light. She was the reason; she was the reason for the T-shirt, the shoes, the jeans, the muscles, and even his new upbeat hip and happy demeanor.

Nyla was this sassy, caramel, brown-skinned, labeled-up diva. I remembered Malik mentioning to me that she worked as a buyer for Saks, and by the looks of her, you could truly tell, because before me stood a couple of Gabriel Union-Dwayne Wade imposters. But it was all good! Nyla was wearing a Chanel scarf wrapped around her long, black, shiny hair with fashionable Marilyn Monroe all-black-everything Prada sunglasses, a sheer-print maxi dress that fit every curve on her body perfectly, with not a bulge or a blemish. She had on rhinestone embellished flat sandals and was holding the new platinum Louis Vuitton handbag, the one I think, Chad Ochocinco may have brought for Evelyn, *back in the day.* I just felt refreshed looking at her. She spoke with such class; you could tell she was well educated and slightly uppity, standing there looking like a bag of money in Rick Ross's voice and postured up like Jennifer on *Basketball Wives.* She was a black Barbie in Jimmy Choo shoes, driving a drop-top Benz with a black Ken on her arm. *You go, girl* was all I could say to myself.

Not only was Nyla fly, but she was fly with brains, attitude and booty. I couldn't believe it, but I was impressed. She had Jamal by the balls too; he was running around behind her like a sick puppy. He did everything for her, except lick the BBQ sauce off her fingers. I had never seen Jamal in this state before, especially not when he was engaged to Paris. Then too, I could see why. Paris was boring; her conversation was boring, her clothes were boring, her hair was boring, that minivan she drove was definitely boring...Hell, even her lipstick and toenail polish were boring. She was just a boring chick, and now that I think about it, that's probably what made Jamal so boring. They say you become what you are around the most.

Paris was also very laid-back and passive. She never really demanded much from Jamal or their relationship, for that matter. She never voiced her opinion about anything other than the color of the curtains or the way she wanted the towels folded after doing the laundry. Paris was more of a *whatever you do is OK with me* type of chick—the overly obedient fiancée (and yes, there is such a thing), and that's where she went wrong. Every man likes a little challenge. Anytime a woman lets her man do whatever he wants, whenever he wants, and just sits back looking boring and being boring, thinking that being quiet and passive is the key to making their relationship last, this is what will happen; especially if he ain't made it official. Putting a ring on it and not making it official, still leaves the door open for intruders.

You will end up losing what you thought you were working so hard to keep and won't even have a clue that it's gone until it's too late, and that will be after he's dropped you for what he really wanted all along. You will be so busy down on the floor trying to pick up and gather all the pieces of yourself back together, life by then will have passed you by, and you'll be lost in trying to find out how you got there. Meanwhile, your ex-fiancé or man will be laid up with a bad bitch like Nyla, who's the absolute opposite of everything you tried so hard to be.

I can sit back and think about this now with a smile, because Nyla and I turned out to be the best of friends; hell, she's my son's godmother. I now know her as a person and not a stereotype based on emotions and/or the situation that went down between Jamal and Paris. One thing I've learned from this whole ordeal is that you should never judge a book by its cover; always take time to read the fine print because not everything is what it appears to be. When you're on the outside looking in, you can't always hear what's being said on the inside.

Just because Jamal was cheating on Paris with Nyla doesn't make Jamal or Nyla out to be bad people. Yeah, maybe both Jamal and Nyla could have gone about it in a more conservative and respectable way, but we all know that sometimes shit just happens. How conservative and re-spectable can you possibly be when you've falling in love with someone else, while in a relationship with another person? I mean, to be honest that was Paris's fault; she had all those babies but didn't make him com-mit. He would have had to marry me, if I was Paris. *Paris, running around playing house and done got kicked out the house, where they do that at?* In situations like Jamal's and Paris's, someone's bound to get hurt, and that someone will be the person you're no longer in love with; which in this case was Paris.

Sometimes in life you have to make moves and adjustments that may not be feasible for both parties, and sometimes those moves and adjust-ments may have bad timing and be uncomfortable. That's when you have to be honest with yourself and make a choice, based on what brings added joy to your life, and what's best for you and not what's considered to be politically correct.

Yeah, Jamal should have probably married Paris, but he didn't be-cause she was too passive and too comfortable with their situation, and maybe if they had been married, he would not have left like that, because he would have had a bigger responsibility to stay. But because Paris didn't put the pressure on and I guess Nyla did, he had to make a decision, and his decision was Nyla.

That said, sometimes you just have to do it and move on, and that's exactly what I think happened with Jamal. He made his choice; he did it and moved on. Unfortunately, Paris was the person left hurting, but I'm willing to bet a million dollars to a sack of donuts, that the signs were there; I believe it was much deeper than Jamal just staying out at night and cheating. That more than likely was at the tail end of it all—you know, the end when you can't do anything else to make the other person leave you, so you just start crying out through your actions, saying, "It's over, let me go, I can't do this or you anymore." Some people just won't let go, they like to hold on until the last second and refuse to see the obvious, knowing that the show was already over and these were just the credits playing.

I may never know exactly what happened with Jamal and Paris that killed their relationship. I may even have my own little theory about what

I think happened, just as everybody else does. But what I do know is that Nyla was not the cause of their breakup. Nyla just happened to be right where Jamal needed her to be and at that same time Jamal was in position to receive what he needed.

*While life may sometimes seem unfair, there are no coincidences or mistakes. Everything happens for a reason; the reason may not seem clear at first, and it may even be hard for you to understand why you're going through certain things, but believe me when I say, there is a point to everything you go through. It may take years of configuration, but eventually it will become clear to you and you'll get the point. Sometimes the point may even work out in your favor, but what's meant to be will be. And the only person that has control over that is someone bigger then us.*

Nyla and Jamal have been married for about nine years now. In that time Jamal has matured and transformed into a whole new species of man—a man who has grown to be responsible for his family's well-being including his boys he had with Paris, who are now off in college and calling Nyla Mom. He has grown financially by opening up his own men's boutique barber salon—of course Ny thought of that. And most of all he's grown spiritually by accepting Jesus Christ as his personal Savior. Becoming a minister and spending time in the Word of God and allowing God to teach him how to be responsible for his actions, and how to love his wife, and in turn teaching that to his boys. He no longer hangs out all night with the guys, getting drunk in bars, like Malik. He goes home to someone he loves, who gives him the drive and purpose, to be a better person from the inside out. Someone who is so important to his life and the man that he has become; that he's asked her to marry him all over again next year for their tenth-year anniversary.

So maybe Jamal and Nyla were already in the plan long before Jamal and Paris. Paris may have even been in the plan the whole time —the plan to lead Jamal to Nyla, as well as the plan that led Nyla to me. You know, the smart sister I never had.

I always find myself sitting back thinking and laughing about that day at the cookout and how Nyla and I connected. Once the ice was broken and my guard was down, we sat there all night eating BBQ and getting tipsy off lemon drop martinis and Manajatwa red wine, just laughing and talking.

Once I started communicating with her and getting to know her better, I realized that we had more in common than I could have ever imagined. Her grandfather was the pastor of the church that my mother grew up in as a child, and now her father has taking over the ministry and is the current head pastor and Jamal is the co-pastor. *Yes!* The home-wrecker is a preacher's kid. Before I knew it that night; me and that home-wrecking husband thief were cackling like hens, making plans to go to church and out for Sunday brunch the next day. And now we are inseparable BFFs.

I often wonder what my life would be like now, if Jamal had never left Paris and met Nyla. It's funny, because back when Paris was calling Malik's house all upset and looking for Jamal, I never would have thought in a million years that all of that, would have had an effect on my life too. In my heart I truly believe Nyla was heaven-sent to Jamal because Jamal needed a woman like her to become the man he is now. Sometime God tends to shake things up a little bit, only to work out all the kinks, in order to make us better people and to bring us closer to Him.

# 7

## Shot Straight through the Heart

While walking up the stairs to my office—something I hardly ever do, but since I didn't work out this morning, I decided to take the stairs—I started checking my voice-mail messages on my cell phone. I notice I have a message from Nyla, sent yesterday at 6:30 p.m. From the sound of her voice, it seems to be rather urgent.

"E, this is Ny."

Call me back as soon as you get this message. I have to talk to you." Confused, I thought, *Yesterday? How did I miss her call, and why didn't I see it this morning when I checked my phone?* Then I realized that she had called after six, so I would have been at Drake's by then. With all the calling Malik did, his calls probably overflowed the phone and kicked hers off. *Dang, I hope there's nothing wrong. I hope she's OK. I wonder if she's gotten the message I left for her earlier. If she did, why hasn't she called me back yet?*

Anxiously I call her again. *Ring, ring, ring, ring.* All music but no answer. *Ooh, her and this "There's Hope" ring tone, I love India Arie but not right now; right now she needs to pick up the phone; how about, I'll thank God for that. What the hell is going on with her?* I hang up.

Suddenly my phone rings right back, as I'm approaching my office. I answer, and can hardly catch my breath from those steps.

"E! What's up? It's Ny."

"What's up with me?" I say, sounding totally out of breath. "No, what's up with you? You got me worried sick. I got your message and it sounded urgent. Are you OK? Where have you been? I've been calling you all morning."

"E, calm down; I'm fine. Are you at work or at the gym? You sound like you are on the treadmill."

"Yeah, I'm at work, I took the stairs. You must have not gotten my message I left for you. I'm just walking through the door. Why?"

"Why didn't you call me back yesterday, and no, I haven't checked my messages today yet," Nyla says.

"I didn't know you called; I'm just getting your message this morning, just a second ago. Anyway, girl, I had no time to call you yesterday. I was with Drake, getting wrapped up, tied up, and sexed up. Until I was rudely interrupted by Malik; with his call-stalking self, ringing my phone off the hook, but that's a whole other story. Why? What's up? Why were you sounding so urgent on your message yesterday? You sounded like something was wrong, but now you're fine? I'm confused."

"E, girl, I have so much to tell you and I don't even know how to get it all out. You're not going to believe this mess. You need to leave work as soon as you can and meet me at Café Z. This is some crazy mess, and I really need to talk to you about it."

"Hold up, so something is going on!"

I say with excitement in my voice. "What's going on; are you pregnant? Are you and Jamal about to make me a godmother, finally?"

"Look, E I don't want to discuss it over the phone. Just come meet me; but to answer your question, *heck no, I'm not pregnant!* Girl, I work too hard on this body for that. We have two kids already and that's enough, so no, you are not about to become a godmother. This crap; is far more fatal than that and bring your stupid stick, because we may need to use it."

"OK, OK, OK. I'm on my way now!"

I don't know who butt we about to tap, but they in trouble now—got me all wired up, grabbing my stupid stick, that I carry for protection when I'm running the park ; *just in case some crazy, stupid person, wanna run-up to get knocked-out.* Leaving work and stuff. I just walked up a whole, three flights of stairs to get here, and now I got to walk back down to leave. *These red bottoms ain't made for walking and most definitely not fighting, I hope I got some tennis or flip-flops in the car.*

I pull up in front of Café Z, a local hot spot for the latest coffee sensations. I park my car and walk in the door, stupid stick in hand, desperately looking around for Ny. I see her sitting over in the corner, in the back, by the window. I throw my hand up to wave so she notices me. *Well, she looks OK,* I think. She's not wearing any shades, so whatever Jamal did, at least it's not visible. It doesn't look like she has a black eye or anything, so what the heck could be so urgent? She say she not pregnant; what else could it be? Oh my God! Did she find out Jamal is on cheat-repeat? Sometimes how you get 'em is how you lose 'em; no shade; *I'm just say!* Or could it be worse? Could it be that he is a down-low brother? So that's what the UNPREDICTABLE T-shirt was all about back in the day. *Oh no! The devil done got a hold to our ministers too,* I think sarcastically. *Now that would deserve a good old-fashioned stupid-stick ass whooping right there! Let this fool be trying to come out of the closet on my friend, talking about he's a gay, ordained minister!*

As I approach her table, she stands up to give me a hug.

"Hey, lady," Nyla says, sounding really dreary.

"Dang; that was dry!" I say. "Are you OK? You know you can talk to me about anything. You're my girl and I got your back on whatever. We all got some skeletons, you know."

"What?" she says, looking really confused. "Yeah, I know you do, but I'm good; how about you? How are things going with you and the family?"

"I'm OK, and the kids are great; but I'd be doing much better if you would tell me why you're sounding so dry, like you just lost your puppy and why I needed to break out the stupid stick. What is all this about? And by the way, I'm working on my skeletons. I just need a little more time, *In Jesus name!*"

"Well, it may be something or it may really be nothing, just something that's been going on for a while, and I just wanted to talk to you about it. And when I asked how was the family; that includes Malik too, he is still your husband, and E! *You can keep playing with Jesus if you want to.* One day, you may really need to call on His name, and He may not answer you, because he'll think you're playing, as usual."

"Nyla, please stop going around the problem. You had me leave work, bring this stick, and you said you had to talk to me ASAP. What is going on? What's up? You always got to throw the *husband* word around and ain't nobody playing with *Jesus!*" I throw up my hand as if to say *whatever.*

"OK E, I'm just going to say it. You said you were with Drake yesterday, right?"

"Yeah, I was with him, why? Did Malik call you looking for me or something, with his crazy, will-call-anybody-to-find-me self?"

"No, Eva, that's not it. You know if that had happened, I would have come by Drake's and picked your behind up. I'm talking about Drake. This has nothing to do with Malik...Well, it does because he's mixed up in this love square by default, so this portion of the mess, doesn't directly involve him, but then again, it does."

"Hold up. Did you say love square? You mean triangle and don't try to make me feel bad. Who you rolling with, me or Malik? Now I'm confused. Me or Malik?" I say again, waiting on her to answer. "You know what; you are really starting to act like your husband. I thought he was trying to act like you, but here lately the script has flipped. *Now, you always preaching!* So I guess you done got ordained too; I guess now the whole family ministers?" I say in an irritated and aggressive tone.

"Look, Ny, I love you to death, but I'm not for all the preaching today—all that holier-than-thou preaching," I say. "Girl, don't start today with this God stuff and I'm gone burn in hell stuff, and the Word of the Lord said stuff."

"First of all, I know what I said," Nyla says. "I said love square, and believe me; a Spellman graduate knows the difference between a triangle and a square; a triangle has three sides and a square has four. And as far as my husband and his preaching, people like you and Drake; y'all need to be the first ones in line to hear the Word, especially Drake. And as far as me starting to act like my husband, don't hate because now I know better. Once you know better, you do better, but some people: like yourself; just can't let go of sin, they actually like it.

"They misinterpret love for lust and sin for actually living. But since I'm the only one here who understands the concept of what I'm talking about, I'll get back on the subject at hand that you are more familiar with. "So, since you tried to go in on me and my husband, OK, let's go in.

"See, what you don't understand is that you and Drake, y'all playing with fire, and somebody's gone get burned. You see, the devil is hot and on the loose, looking to burn some dumb, naïve, suckers like y'all right on up. He likes to dangle carrots of attraction to lure you into his world, but the catch is that he doesn't show you the full picture. He just gives you excerpts of the parts that look good. That said, did Drake tell you anything or talk to you about anything yesterday?"

"No. And why you getting all upset and whipping me with your Bible? You know I don't like playing with God like that. I love the Lord and one day he is going to save me from myself; I was just kidding about your preaching husband. Man, you sure do love that man. You take everything about him so personal. Loosen up. I can't even joke about him. And what's up with this square, devil, carrot, picture stuff you talking about, 'cause now you saying too much and getting too deep; it ain't even that serious. Why would Drake need to talk to me about something? You know us and how we do it. We were so busy doing what we do; we really didn't have any time for conversation. The only conversation we had was called body language, and my body was screaming Drake...Drake...Drake, and his body was singing E-E-E!" I say with a huge smile on my face.

Nyla, just looked at me in shame and shook her head, and said. "Help her Lord!"

"Anyway...So, how are you guys doing? You know; you and Drake and y'all's situation. Has he been bugging you lately about spending more time with him or questioning you about Malik? And what are you planning on doing about your marriage?"

"No, not really," I say. "He'll say sarcastic stuff every now and then, but he hasn't been pressuring me like he used to. He's beginning to understand my situation more and more, especially because of the kids and all. He respects my decision regarding that, as well as what he and I have together. Why? Everything seems to be pretty cool with Drake and me; I mean, we have our time together and we use that time wisely. But for real, Ny: what are all the ninety-nine Drake questions about?"

"Well, E, I have something to tell you I think you should know, so let me talk, say what I have to say, and you just do the impossible and listen for once. OK. First, I want to start off by saying that I'm not telling you this for any other reason, than for you to be up on whatever is going on, if indeed there is something going on. So don't kill the messenger, but don't get it twisted. By no means am I saying that what you and Drake are doing is OK. But because you are my girl and I love you so much, even though this man got you acting like someone I don't even know right now, I still got your back. Just like you came with the stupid stick without a question asked, I'm coming with my Bible, and whatever support you need; no questions asked."

I just sit there with a blank stare, heart beating fast like I just ran a red light on Tucker.

"What I'm about to say may have some truth, or it may just be gossip, considering Drake has become so popular with his second restaurant/club, The D Spot Too opening and all and was featured in Deluxe Magazine."

"Hold up, stop, Ny. What are you talking about?" I say.

"Just shut up and let me finish, please," says Ny. "Man, can you ever just be quiet and listen?" *I see why China didn't want to tell you.* "What I was about to say is that I spoke with China yesterday. Did you know she's been kicking it with one of Drake's good friends? You probably know the guy, his name is Ellis. Really nice looking, dark-skinned, light-brown eyes, about six foot two. He's a record producer and works for a label here in the Lou. No; I take that back. He actually owns his own record label—nothing big but from what I hear, he is about to blow up or something like that. I've only met him once."

"Get to the damn point, Ny!" I say with urgency in my voice. "And what do you mean; China didn't want to tell me?"

"Didn't I just say don't kill the messenger? Dang, girl, shut up. I'm getting to the point and don't curse at me. I have to give you the backdrop first. Now let me finish the darn story. Man E, is it that hard for you just to shut up and listen? Now I see what Malik be talking about; you just won't let people talk. You always have to have the first and the last word all the time. Stop cutting me off."

"Whatever, come on, girl," I say.

"Thank you! Anyway, before I was rudely interrupted again, what I was getting to is that China stated that they all went out one night."

"Who is they all, and what does this have to do with me?" I say, real confused.

"OMG! E, shut up; I'm getting to that; China said that they went out—her, Ellis, and another one of Ellis's male friends. She said Ellis and his friend were going on and on about college, and how they all shared a dorm room together and—"

"And can you get to the point? Just say it," I say with frustration in my voice.

"OK, heffa! Since you really want to know and can't listen to the whole story without cutting me off, here it is in the flesh unfiltered, 'cause you know all about living in the flesh unfiltered; *right!* China said Ellis said Drake has a baby on the way, by some girl who went to college with them. That the girl just moved back to St. Louis last year. Something about she moved to LA, after college to focus on her singing career, but apparently it didn't jump off the way she wanted it to, so she ended up coming back here to hook up with Ellis to see if he could help her.

"From what I hear, she's been here for a year or so and during that time, she hooked up with not only Ellis, but also with Drake, and they have been kicking it nonstop. She's supposed to be the lead singer of some group Ellis produces or something like that. She's also supposed to be about four months pregnant—pregnant by Drake; so no! You are not going to be a godmother by me but you're going to be a fictitious step-mother by Drake. *There!* Is that to the point enough for you? *Can you hear me now?!"* Nyla says sarcastically.

"What!" I say, totally disturbed and confused; anger and disbelief in my voice. "What do you mean she supposed to be about four months pregnant by Drake? What Drake? Not my Drake, *I'm sure.* And who is this bitch again, and where did she come from? Did you Google this ho? Give me my purse so I can Facebook or Google this tramp from my phone. I don't give a damn about her wanting to be an *American Idol* reject with a failed career. Who the hell is she and where did she come from again? My brother Ronnie lives in LA; I'll call him, and see if he knows her!

Oh hell no! Call China. Did China get her full name? Where is China? Is she with this Ellis dude now? Call her. No, that's OK, I'll call her, because we both know sometimes it's hard for you to interpret a mass amount of information at once, especially when China is telling the story. That girl be all over the place. She can't get her own life story right, so how she gone tell somebody else's? One minute you say this Ellis guy is a producer; then you say he owns his own record label *or something like that!* Is that what you said, or is that what China said or what she thinks she knows? Do you even know, because you are confusing me? I need to talk to China, and China needs to call Ellis so I can hear this shit straight from him."

*Right now I'm in a rattling and raving state of mind.*

"Plus Ny, I ain't even never heard of no dude named Ellis, and I know all Drake's close friends, just like he know y'all, and this Ellis dude ain't ringing no bells, and when did you meet him and where was I?"

"Whoa, kemosabe. Slow down there, Mrs. Thing. I may not be the best interpreter in the world for Spain, but I'm cool in the United States and I'm not stupid by far. See, the difference between you and me is that I know how to shut up and listen when it's necessary. You don't. Now look E, I know there is probably nothing else I can say right now to convince you, but I know what China told me, and I know you're acting real crazy and naïve right now. Do you have amnesia? Because apparently you must have forgotten that you are a married woman—married to Malik, not to Drake. You cannot go around calling people, asking them to air someone else's laundry!

"Like you said, you don't even know this Ellis guy, never heard of him. Have you ever thought that maybe this is the reason why you don't know him? Maybe Drake didn't want you to know him because of this little chick he dealing with. You don't know Ellis, just like you apparently don't know Drake or this chick who is supposed to be pregnant by him. But you do know China, and she happens to be one of your closest friends, and you cannot get her all involved in this mess. She is looking out for you; you can't bust her out like that by having her call Ellis and acting all weird and crazy. Plus, you know China is not the type to be running her mouth about some nonsense talk, unless there's a good reason. And this reason is as good as any because it involves you.

"Besides, Ellis apparently knows nothing about an Eva. But isn't that the way you and Drake wanted it? Where no one knows but you two? Do you think that if this guy, Ellis, knew about you and Drake, he would have been running off at the mouth like that around China? No!

"Eva, I don't know if you have lost your mind or what type of spirit has invaded it, but I want the real Eva back, the one who has common sense. You and Drake are living a lie, a secret; a secret lie, whether it's clear to you or not. No one knows what you and Drake have going on together but you and Drake. *Oh! And the Lord*, but that's a whole other issue.

"I'm your girl and to be honest, I really don't know, what's going on with you and Drake. I only know what you tell me about y'all's situation, and that's that you say you love Drake and he probably loves you back, but let's be realistic. Stop and think for a moment. You're married, regardless of the issues going on in it; you're still married, and do you honestly think, this man is satisfied with the relationship or arrangement you all have? For real? Really satisfied!

"Do you think he's so satisfied with a few hours a week, maybe a few more if he's lucky, that he does not think about or want to see anyone else and/or have a real relationship with anyone else? E, if you thought for one second that Drake was only screwing you for a few hours a week and not screwing anyone else, you need serious counseling, and I'm about to call Wendy Williams to put you on the hot topic-hot mess segment. What the heck? Have you let this man flip the script on you? Now you're looking crazy, cuckoo for Cocoa Puffs.

"I promise you, I don't know what has attached itself to you, but what I do know is that you need to shake it off and find out where your loyalty lies. That should be with your family, not with a man who's about to start his own. To be honest, E, I like Drake. Don't get me wrong, I think you guys could have made the cutest couple; fifteen years ago. But dang, E, not now; it's not y'all's time, and right now this thing y'all have going on is no good for you or him, considering you have a full-fledged family at home, not to mention a vow with God. Everything that is good to you is not good for you and vice versa, especially when it can damage you and other people in the process.

"What gets me is that Drake didn't even have the decency or the courage to tell you about it; you had to hear it through the ghetto-vine. But you guys have such a connection...connection, my behind, that's an illegal soul tie, if you ask me! You can't have a connection if the phone isn't plugged up, and y'all ain't married, so y'all ain't plugged. So what that leaves you with is a phone that you can't even use and no communication because there never was a connection. Even if this is true, who can you call to clean it up? You better be trying to call on Jesus, for real this time, and ask for forgiveness for your wrongdoing in this situation and ask Him to clean you up, not this mess and most definitely not Drake."

Nyla is obviously upset and furious, looking at me in pity and shaking her head.

"E, if I haven't learned anything in my relationship with Jamal, I've learned that you have to live in appreciation for what you have, and if and when it's time for you to move on and do something else, God will move you," she says. "But you cannot move yourself, 'cause if you do, you will only mess things up, worse than what they already are.

"I know you remember how Jamal and I got together; do you think that was easy? That Paris situation was a mess, Eva. Even after we got married, it still was a thorn in my side. The only thing that kept us together was the God in us. *Now*, I can sit here and say that everything worked out for the good. But in the beginning; it was hell: a hell that we had created for ourselves, all because we didn't let God handle it. It took us years of counseling, to get where we are today. So don't look at me, as this Bible toting chick, with the perfect marriage and no flaws. It's God that keeps us E, not us alone. Once you fully understand that, your life will be so much easier to manage.

"So, this baby-on-the-way thing is not saying move forward; it's saying fall back and appreciate what you have. It's a sign, E. Please pay attention. God is not done with you and/or Malik yet, 'cause believe me, when He is, you will know."

All I can do is sit there. For once in my life, I am speechless. There is nothing for me to say. What can I say after all that? Is there even anything to be said? I knew that bitch Karma was real and that she would find me one day, and when she did, I would have to pay—pay for all those hours, all those lies, all those after-work creeps along with all my indiscretion and deceptions. I just didn't know it would be this costly. No one ever does.

I sit in a daze for about three minutes, staring straight ahead in a state of shock. Isolation is felt across the table. I'm blocking everything and everyone out, not hearing, not seeing, and not caring. My throat feels like I've just swallowed a glass of nails. I'm trying to hold back the tears, but I can't, and they just come tumbling down, like an avalanche of rocks. I can't believe what I've just heard. I can't begin to imagine Drake with another woman—holding hands, kissing, dancing, making love, giving everything away that I have claimed as mine. Then to have a family in the making that doesn't include me? *What kind of man is he?*

And even though Nyla has read me my rights in a biblical sense, I still don't get it. I still don't get that I am living a life of sin that can either take me down or build me up. My only concern is still Drake and this love triangle—I mean, square that I'm in.

"Eva, Eva, E. Are you OK?" Nyla says, grabbing me by the hand.

"Oh, Ny, I'm sorry. I must have blacked out for a minute. I'm fine; Drake was just something to do anyway. You know, just something to get me through everything I was going through with Malik. I'm ready to go." I reach for my purse to get a tissue. As I wipe the tears from my face, I say. "I have to get back to the office and do some things, so how about I call you later on this evening?" I stand up, trying to act as if I am cool.

Nyla stands up, directly in front of me, grabs both of my hands and say. "E, I just want you to know that I am here for you, and although I may not have agreed or understood your relationship with Drake, I had to respect it because you are my friend. But at the same time I have to look out for your best interest and speak the truth in everything; that goes for me and China both. You are our girl, and we don't want to see you upset and hurt, especially not over something that really doesn't even belong to you. China didn't know how to tell you, and that's why she asked me to talk to you. So clean your face and don't you feel bad; everything will be OK and work itself out. Note this in your journal as a lesson learned."

"Ny, I'm not upset, I'm just disappointed. I'll be OK. Just pray for me— now, I need to get back to work because I have a lot of work to do. I'm not tripping off this crap. It is what it is. I have a husband and two lovely kids at home, so I'm good. Shoot, people want to be me. I have it all: a good job, great friends, and a prestigious family. I'm cool. Plus, anyway, Drake was just a toy for me to play with, and like all toys, you play with them until they break down and/or lose value or sometimes, you just get tired of them or grow out of them, so you stop playing with them and move on to something else."

Ny just stands there listening to me go on and on with nonsense about Drake being my toy. She really knows better; hell she knows me better than I know myself sometimes, but she just let me vent and have my moment, like a true friend does.

"E, as your friend, I'm worried about you. Will you please do me a huge favor?"

"What, Ny?"

"Please, don't feed off into any of this mess. Realize what you have in real life. You said it yourself: women would love to be in your shoes. You have a wonderful life. A lot of women would kill to have the life you have, and your life will be even better with Drake out of it. Let Drake go. Just let him go and move on. I know you say you love him, but for once think about your family first, and if not them, think about you.

"You and Drake have had your season, now it's time to move on. Focus and realize that nothing lasts forever, unless there are vows involved, and sometimes those fail. But when you are in a marriage, you are in the will of God, and if you ask for help and let Him in the equation, He will hold it all together. But you have to let Him in first. This is your chance to release yourself from Drake's bondage. God is giving you a way of escape. Let Drake go; he is just a bad habit you are going to have to break. After all, if you stopped drinking, I know you can kick the Drake habit.

"Go home, Eva; since you've already taken off from work for the day, go home to your family who loves you and ask God to fix your marriage. Also ask Him for forgiveness and the power to let go. Once your heart has been set free and your head is clear, you'll be OK. Stop choosing Drake; it's time to choose your family and work on your marriage."

On that note, I throw the money on the table for the bill and begin to walk out of the café. Nyla follows behind me as I walk to my truck, still talking. At this point I'm about to go insane. I can't take another healthy word from her. She may have the perfect marriage, but I don't, and it didn't start falling apart when Drake came into the picture. It was falling apart way before that.

*Yeah! Sure! Women want to be in my shoes and have my life; that's because it looks good. A lot of shoes look good, but once in them, will you be able to walk and stand in them, is the question. I just like to say that; to make people think it's all good, but for real; I hate these shoes, and this life... is hell!*

She's getting on my freaking nerves with her feelings and concerns, going on and on about me trying to stay strong and asking me to please go home to my family and pray and ask God to forgive me. How about Malik needs to be on his knees before me, how about I'm the victim? He created this mess, not me. I want to just yell, *"Not now, Ny,"* and say, *"Shut the fuck up,*" but I guess she is doing what any good friend would do in a situation like this. But right now I have too many things distracting and disturbing my mind. I can't comprehend anything she's saying. Even if I could, right now I don't want to, because I'm not interested.

Right now I'm frantically upset and angry, and I don't need to hear that uppity, sanctified, Stepford Wives bull crap. It may sound insane, but what I need right now, right at this moment, is a glamour-ghetto, hood chick like my stylist Zoe B, who will jump in my truck with me and go track a ho down, kick ass, and ask questions later. Preferably Drake's, but his pregnant tramp would do just fine. Ooooh! Drake is lucky that Zoe is out of town, 'cause it wouldn't be anything for me to call her and go pick her up. And we would ride down on his ass. *Yes, I am a little ghetto too. There is still some Peabody-hood residue down in me, especially when it comes to somebody playing games with me like this.*

# 8

## Babies Aren't for Us Blues

*I* am distraught. Everything just seems so vague and unclear to me. I could have waited on this baby-mama-drama bull crap for another day. How can this be happening to me? Bull-crap baby mamas are not in the plan. In a matter of hours, my whole future has been wrecked, wrecked with words I can't bear to face. I'm so far from where I was two hours ago that it seems unreal; I'm so confused about Drake and our relationship right now, I don't even know what to think. My mind and body have become limp. I'm trying to be tough, but I feel weak and hollow from the inside out. I feel like a beat-up, bruised piece of fruit that's been left to rot. Although I have yet to know if indeed what I've heard is true, the thought alone torches my heart.

But, I must save face, though, and fake it and play the role with Nyla like I'm OK, or else she will never leave and let me go. I've got stuff to do—people to call, questions to ask—and I can't concentrate on what I need to do first if she doesn't shut up and leave. She's only making me feel worse with all this "everything will work out, pray on it" BS. I need results now!

I've already taken off from work, so that will give me some extra time; but first I need to try to contact Drake. *Man! I'm thinking. Would Nyla please leave and carry her butt on somewhere! Why is she walking me to my truck? I know how to get to it, open the door, and get in on my own. I'm a grown woman. Man! She is really going overboard.*

I play it off and get into my truck and tell Nyla thanks for everything. I tell her I don't feel well; I say my head is hurting, and I'm going to take her advice and go home and lie down. *Hell if I am!*

I tell her I will call her later once I wake up and not to call me, because I need some me time alone to help me relax—*anything to make her shut up, get in her car, and leave.* She has gotten on my nerves for real this time; I know she's only trying to help and be a good, supportive friend, but I think she's forgotten that she too, had the option to let go. While she just went through this whole spill, about her and Jamal's situation, in the beginning and how hard it was; it sounded good. But she still had the option, to let go and she didn't.

So, while she's telling me to let Drake go. I have to hold my tongue because I almost told her something; believe me, she would not have liked it. I almost told her that, *maybe if she would have let Jamal go, he'd be married to Paris instead of her right now, and that, that would have made everything much easier, for Paris.* Nyla of all people should know that, letting go is easier said than done.

But then, I have to understand that she is only being a caring friend, and after all, saying that and trying to hurt her feelings, wouldn't have helped mine; she's not Drake nor is she the tramp who's supposed to be pregnant by Drake. She's my best friend who's just trying to keep me on my square and get me out of one.

Finally she kisses me on my cheek and tells me for the fifth time to go home, pray, and take it easy, and that everything is going to be OK. She closes my door and starts to walk away towards her car. I want to pick up my cell phone so bad, my hand is twitching, but I know Nyla is going to look back. If she sees me on the phone, she'll automatically know who I'm calling. She knows me well enough to know that if I'm on the phone that quick, I'm trying to call Drake, which would mean I'm not on my way home to lie down; I'm on my way to start some problems and get myself in some more mess.

I turn my car on to let her know I'm about to pull off and leave. I pull down the visor to look into the mirror and act like I'm fixing my hair and makeup to throw her off so she will leave before me. Yes, she finally pulls off, blows her horn, waves bye, and leaves. I wait a few more minutes, until she is out of sight.

"Thank goodness!" I say out loud as I anxiously reach for my cell phone; I grab it out of my purse, furiously thinking, *how do I approach this? What do I say? How do I say I found out*? I can't say that China told Nyla and Nyla told me. That wouldn't be cool; that wouldn't look appealing to Ellis on China's behalf, and we'd all look like a bunch of gossiping housewives or worse, Peter, Cynthia's husband on *Real Housewives of Atlanta*.

Should I even call him? Maybe I should just send a text message. No, that's not personal enough. I need him to hear the hurt in my voice. *Dang!* What do I do?

I decide to call. My fingers are numb, my palms are sweating, and my mind is scattered with mumbled and jumbled-up words that probably won't even come out right, but I'm calling. I start to dial; my heart racing like it does when I hear Malik's ring tone when I'm with Drake. *Ring, ring, ring…*"Pick up, you A-hole," I say to myself.

Then I hear, "You have reached the Sprint PCS phone of 314-621-5039. Press one to leave a message." *Dang it! What should I do now? Should I leave a message; what should I say*? Then without thinking, voice sounding fidgety and nervous, I say, "Hey, this is me. Give me a call as soon as you get this message. It's urgent." I hang up. Within a second of the hang-up, I can't hold back any longer. I start to cry, thinking, *What will happen after this, after he calls me back and confirms that what I've heard is true, and how will he tell me? What will he say? Will he lie, or will he be the man I know him to be and tell me the truth, regardless of the consequences that will follow? Or does he think there will be no consequences, considering I have issues myself with my marriage and all? What will happen to us, to our arrangement?*

*I wonder where I will go to release from a long week of stress. Will I still have my hours and my days, or will I be banded because of his new life, his new child, and possibly his new wife?*

*Does he love her? Does he really love me like he says he does, and if he does, why would he keep this away from me? But more than that, why would he do this to me?*

*I wonder if he's with her now. Is that why he didn't answer? Are they at the doctor's office, doing the new baby ultrasound thing together? What has happened? Is this the last chapter to our romance novel? How could he ruin something as perfect as what we have together, with this?*

All sorts of crazy thoughts and questions are running through my head. I am literally tripping.

I glance up at the clock on my dash and realize I have been sitting in this truck for over thirty minutes tripping, thinking, daydreaming, crying, listening to Nancy Wilson, inhaling every sensual sound of her voice, classifying every song she sings as a part of me and my life. Tears stream down my face, dripping, dropping onto my heart, every drop sizzling like water hitting hot grease. I am hurt.

I am so hurt and so crushed that I have to turn the radio off; I just can't listen anymore. I have been dropped like a hot potato, without a clue of how I got on the floor—left to pick myself up and piece myself all back together, by a man who is invisible to my everyday life. What was I thinking?

OMG, I'm Paris!

I promised myself as a young girl that I would never be the kind of woman who allowed a man to do this to her, but I've become the woman I promised myself I would never be—a woman who has put all her trust into a man. And in this case, knowing that he wasn't even really mine anyway is even more devastating.

I really need to see Drake *right now*! I need to speak with him, I need to hear him say that this is all a lie and that I am his only girl, while kissing me and caressing my body against his, under those Egyptian cotton sheets, in his Neo-Soul, behind those frosted glass doors. I need to see the smile that brightens my day, those big, bold, marble eyes that intoxicate my mind. I want to hear his moans and feel his groans that tingles my womb with every touch, then fall asleep and wake up in his arms, realizing this was all a dream, all a lie. Just a figment of my imagination.

I need Drake to soothe my pain, even if he may have caused it. I need to be rescued from this awful vision of deception on his part, before the picture is finished being painted in my mind and can't be restored.

I'm feeling abandoned and alone, just as I did as a child. The feelings I felt as a young girl have met up with me again! I need to be in his presence. I need his love to help me through this. How is it that the person who caused the pain is the only person who can cure it? I run to Drake when I need to get away from all the hurt and confusion of my life. How can he be the one who has caused it? How?

This is insane; I'm going insane, with all these scrambled thoughts and emotions dancing in my head. Nyla may be right; maybe I do need to go home and lie down and try to look beyond what has been said to me today. At least until I hear from Drake. My mind is on Drake overload, thinking and thinking and trying to figure out what is going on and what this will mean for me.

I know I need the strength to let go and the courage to move forward with my real life and my marriage, but the pain keeps me sitting right here, stuck in this truck, tripping and trying to figure out why I'm so hurt over something that is only a part of my life a few hours a week.

"OK, E, you need to pull it together." I start talking to myself. "You sitting here trip-thinking about Drake, hoping that he'll call. And asking yourself why you let yourself get this involved is not going to change what it is. It's not going to make him call any quicker, nor will it give you any answers, so let it go, and go home like Ny said!"

Once again I have to collect myself, pull it together, and act like an adult who has a husband and family at home. So I follow Nyla's lead, and I ask God to help me. I pray for Him to help me to clear my thoughts, to remove this relationship from my life, to give me strength and peace within myself, and to guide me home to my family, where I belong. In essence I'm thinking God is not going to help me for real, because of all the sinning I've been doing. I'm thinking I probably deserve exactly what I'm getting and that God is probably punishing me for all that I have done in my marriage. How can I even be so bold to ask God for help in a situation like this?

This is nothing but the devil's work, and God doesn't want any part of it. I apologize to God for even asking for help.

I pull out of the parking lot, feeling helpless and hopeless, continuously thinking about everything Nyla told me today, but no longer worrying about it—only feeling concerned about what's to come. Her voice and conversation are bouncing back and forth in my mind like Ping-Pong balls. Then all of a sudden it strikes me that I'm only thinking of myself, not even thinking about Drake.

Has Malik rubbed off on me so much until I've become this selfish little self-centered woman who only cares about her own satisfaction and no one else's? How can I sit here and be so selfish and self-absorbed, only thinking of my needs and wants and what's going to happen to me? This is not just about me; this is much bigger than me. What about Drake? What if what I heard today does have some truth and there really is a baby? This will not only affect me. I'm the last person who should be tripping and worrying. How will this affect Drake? I can't imagine Drake as a father. This means he will have to compromise his wants and needs for the wants and needs of someone other than me: a child, a baby. His baby, plus a baby mama.

Drake is a bachelor at heart; he is his own man. I don't see how a child would fit into his freelance, free-spirited lifestyle. Drake is used to doing what Drake wants to do, when Drake wants to do it, and how Drake wants to do it. Drake's main priorities are his two businesses, hanging out, hooking up with me, and working out. Hell, this is a man who can't even take the time to match up his socks before he puts them on, so how will he adapt to having a real-life human being to take care of? This will be a whole new agenda added to his life, not to mention this woman.

As I jump onto the freeway heading home, so many what-if questions flash through my mind, annoying the mess out of me, that I decide to turn the radio back on to calm my nerves and tune out all the negative thoughts that are crossing my mind. Even before I turn up the volume, I hear it—the voice of an angel and she is right on time.

It's the one song that can break you down and lift you up all in one verse. It's Mariah Carey's "Don't Forget about Us." I start to turn it back off to keep from crying but I can't. I have to listen. I say to myself; *Man, I must have a friend in Tammie Holland, and she must have known I was hurt and going through and played this one just for me.*

I turn it up and just smile; this song is just what I needed at this very moment. Mrs. Mariah was speaking just what was on my mind. I needed to hear those lyrics of possibility... Then the magic verse came—*when it's for real, it's forever, so don't forget about us.* That was all I needed to hear; that one verse set me straight. That told the story. What's that old saying? *Forget what you heard, it's what you know.*

From that song on, all the way home, all I can think are happy thoughts about Drake and me. Once I think about it, I can honestly say that it has truly been a blessing to have known Drake at all—to have had him in my life, whether it was for days, hours, months or years, and to have shared such a sweet romance, is irreplaceable. It has surely been my pleasure because not only has he showed me love, but he also has taught me what true love should feel like. No other man has ever touched my heart the way he has. Just the thought of Drake brings on a glow of light and a feeling of peace for me. This is what love is, and what love is supposed to do. Maybe I've been taking this whole conversation with Nyla all too serious. Maybe I need to cut out all the crying, dry my eyes, and take a moment to think about what I have gained in this relationship rather than what I will be losing, and stop suffocating myself in disappointment. I need to just humble myself and move toward acceptance for whatever the outcome or truth may be. After all, I put my own self in this position and became comfortable in it

Whenever Drake calls, if I find out that all of what was said today is true, the only question I have for him would be: "Do we close our doors to open the new ones, or do we carry on with our pretend world with added additions, your new child and baby mama?"

# 9

## The Day I Met the Perfect Stanger

*I* walk into the house, appreciating how the quietness rings throughout. I glance over at the microwave and notice it's only twelve thirty. *My, my, my,* I think, *this day has really taken a toll on me.* It feels like I've completed a whole eight-hour work shift and it should be going on six in the evening. I flip off my shoes and head straight to the wine caddy in the dining room. I technically have stopped drinking, or so I say, but on a day like today, I need one. Just the sight of the wine, brings on a calm and content, ready-to-relax spirit in me. I know I haven't had a drink in over three years, but hell, I need it today. See, this is when I need Nyla to keep me delivered: at least from something. *Where is she now with the Holy oil and Bible?* She told me a long time ago, once you get delivered from something, you have to remove it, and not to be around it. But did I listen? Nope. Now I'm about to mess up, over three years of being sober over what? A baby mama!

I know Malik will not be home until late tonight because it's Friday, and after work he'll probably go to happy hour with the guys. After having one drink, happy hour won't be enough. He'll need more, so he'll probably keep the party moving and go somewhere else, like across the water to the stripe club or something. *Good*, I think. *I'll be good and drunk and asleep by then, and he will never know; he won't be able to smell the wine on my breath from smelling the Jack on his.* This is great; I need some stress relief, some peace and quiet, and some Eva time anyway.

To add to the glory, it's the kids' weekend with Grandma Mae: Malik's mom, so she will be picking them up from school. That's another distraction eliminated.

"This is marvelous," I say out loud, with a smile beaming across my face. "I guess Nyla's little saying is right, *everything is working out for the good*. I can relax my mind and body in peace, without any added interruptions from the kids or Malik."

I pour myself a glass of wine, and the smell of it brings back a familiar feel-good spirit that quick. As if I didn't already have enough spirits in me.

I start up the stairs to the bedroom, glass in one hand and the bottle in the other, humming Mariah Carey. I mix everything from *The Emancipation of Mimi* to *Butterfly*, thinking, *I could listen to her all night.* I am feeling good; it's like old times. For some reason I am having a familiar feeling of happiness. I walk into the bedroom and go straight to the CD rack, where I start flipping through my CD collection, pulling out every Mariah CD I own. I just put them all in the CD player and select Random.

In the bathroom I place my glass of wine along with the bottle on the table next to the tub—yes, I said. I grab the Laura Mercier, start the water, and let the bubbles begin to flow. I light some candles like it is eight o'clock at night and I've just finished a long day at the office. It's Eva time.

This is how I used to cleanse myself, internally and externally, during the days when Malik was acting a complete fool. This is what I used to do to relax my mind: wine, a hot bath, the scent of Laura, and the sounds of good music. This is where all the negativity and clutter of the world would be suppressed when there was no Drake, so why not see if it still works?

The relaxation of a nice, hot bubble bath always brings me peace of mind, and good music takes me away from my reality; Laura gives me aroma therapy; and the wine, oh the wine, soothes my painful thoughts. Or at least it will help me forget about them for a while, until I sober up. *What made me ever stop drinking?* Oh I know; that doggone Nyla and her preaching husband, telling me that the wine wasn't going to wash the pain away unless it was in Communion. LOL! I laugh at myself.

One foot slides into the tub, then another. I slide my body into the hot steaming water and watch the vapors rise. I lay back, close my eyes, and just exhale and take in the sensual sound of Mrs. Mariah, just relaxing and reminiscing.

Before I know it, I'm pouring a third glass of 1977 Seductivo 750 ML Vintage Merlot, laughing and giggling, thinking about when Drake and I first met. If Malik had walked in on me, lying back in that tub, smiling like that, he would have thought I had company under all those bubbles, the way I was giggling.

It's so funny to me because it's all so clear; I can remember every little detail from A-Z, as if it were just yesterday. How Drake was wheeling and dealing with me all night, without saying a word. By the end of the night, the deal was closed and he had sealed it. With a kiss, I must add.

I can remember not even knowing his name, and now I can't stop saying it. It was about three to four years ago. I was sitting on the back patio of Bar French, waiting on Nyla and China for dinner. All of a sudden, out of nowhere, Drake walked right in front of me, looking like a piece of chocolate eye candy—a piece of creamy Dove Chocolate, the milk chocolate ones in the blue foil, that are so rich and tasty, all you need is one piece, and you're hooked.

At first glance we made eye contact. He looked at me with those big marble eyes and displayed a little smiley smirk with one eyebrow up and one eyebrow down; it was if his eyes were speaking to me, saying, "Hi, how are you? You look nice tonight."

I could not resist that smile or those marble eyes. He was so adorable and cute; he was like a red-bottom black-patent pump—not too over-the-top, just sexy and classic and a lady's must-have.

He captured my attention for the rest of the night, just from that smiley smirk grin he had given me. I sensed a level of confidence from that—not arrogance but confidence. He was a man who was secure with himself and knew what he liked and how to get it.

See, Drake was different. He displayed a different air about himself, different from all the other ten guys who had tried to pursue me that night. I had totally ignored the others without a doubt, but Drake had me curious, curious to know what that air was that made him so different.

I could tell from the way he looked at me that he was interested in me, just as I was in him. So I responded to his invitation. However, being the lady that I am, or should I say the other lady that I can turn into, I responded in a more sensual way. I looked over to where he was sitting and looked him dead in his eyes. Then I lightly lifted my right leg, gently placing it across my left one, seductively crossing them. The movement made the sexy, sassy, fancy, turquoise dress I was wearing rise up, just enough to enhance my thighs and calves.

I could tell that he worked out, and that like me, he was into his body development and physical appearance. So I decided to impress him by letting him know, I worked out as well by showing off the perfect structure of my calf muscles and well-toned thighs. This would show him without saying a word to each other that we already knew we had something in common.

To take it a step further, as I turned to glance at the front door to see if the girls were entering, I stood up and rubbed my thighs up and down in a slow, sensual motion, allowing the silk material of my dress to cling to my body. I guess you could say that I too was feeling flirty as well as confident that night. I knew he was watching; I could feel his gaze on the back of my neck, beaming like rays of sun.

I turned back to pick up my drink and took a quick peek to see if he was still looking. I noticed that he was gone. Nyla and China were walking in from the side door over to the bar where I was sitting, but the Man in the Hat had disappeared from sight. I couldn't even speak to Nyla or China; I was so busy surveying the room, trying to figure out where my red-bottom patent pump had disappeared to so fast. China looked at me, with confusion in her eyes and said, "Did you lose something?"

I can remember plain as day what my exact words were. "Yeah, this adorable red-bottom patent pump, wearing a Burberry House checked hat with big, beautiful marble eyes that just had my panties dancing in the rain."

That's all I could remember about him: his big marble eyes, how cute he looked in that hat, and the tingle he left in my panties with that sexy grin he gave me.

All I could picture in my mind was the Man in the Hat with those big, marble eyes lustfully watching me and that sexy grin teasing me from across the room.

Even after Nyla, China, and I were escorted to our table inside the dining area, I continued to survey the room like an eagle looking for her prey, but there was no sign of him. The Man in the Hat had vanished, but for some reason, I knew just from that brief moment of eye contact, we had made a connection. I felt it, in my soul that we would meet again. It was like he had come to Bar French just for me.

After we finished dinner and were just sitting at the table chatting, Nyla got a call from Diamond, another one of our close friends. Diamond went to college with Nyla at Spellman. Then after Diamond graduated med school, she accepted a job in Atlanta and moved away. This weekend she was in town for a doctor's convention. Although she's constantly traveling back and forth from Atlanta to St. Louis on the regular to visit her boyfriend Conner, who lives here, we don't get to spend a lot of time with her because she's always playing catch-up with Conner. So whenever she's in town and calls us to hang out, we all try to make arrangements to hang out with her before she leaves or goes back into hibernation with Conner.

When Nyla hung up the phone with Diamond, she said Diamond asked us to meet up with her at this new spot called The D Spot. She said she and Conner were there eating and hanging out and she wanted to see us before she left to go home tomorrow. By now we were all full and ready to call it a night and shut it down after having a few cocktails and dinner. But since we knew Diamond was leaving the next day, we decided to go down there and hang out for a little while. Plus, all of us had been hearing all the rave reviews all over town about this new spot—how it was supposed to be the new hot spot in the Lou—so we wanted to check it out to see what all the fuss was about. And what better night than tonight with all the girls, so we all jumped into Nyla's car and headed downtown while I left my car at the restaurant.

When we walked into the spot, just from the décor you could tell it was more of an upscale spot, a bit too upscale for the Lou. It was amazing. It reminded me of a club you would see in Miami or Vegas. Downstairs on the first floor was the club/dance area with several bar areas, and upstairs there was a restaurant soul lounge and an enclosed cigar bar. The décor had a soft contemporary feel with a touch of retro soul; fine pieces of art hung throughout the entire place—John Holyfield's *Jazz Lounge*, Archibald Motley's *Nightlife*, Annie Lee, William Tolliver. I felt like I was at an African art bar exhibit. The art alone was breathtaking, and the club was spectacular.

Right at that very moment, while I was admiring a captivating painting, *Best Friends* by Cbabi Bayoc, and thinking, *man, I need to buy this painting for one of each of my girls as a token of our friendship*, I saw him.

"It's him!" I yelled, looking around to make sure I didn't embarrass myself by being too loud and yelling like I was crazy. I ran over to Diamond and Conner, because I didn't know where Nyla and China had hookered off to and said, "It's the Man in the Hat!"

Both Conner and Diamond looked at me and said, "What? It's who? What are you yelling about?"

"It's the Man in the Hat, from earlier," I said.

Conner looked at me and said, "Where? You saw a celebrity? I knew it." He looked at Diamond and said, "I told you, Diamond, this place is the spot; it's fly as hell in here. I knew there would be some celebrities in here. See, Diamond, you don't have to live in Atlanta to party with celebs. STL is moving on up, ever since Nelly put us on the map."

Looking dazed and confused, I turned around and said, "No, Conner. Not a celebrity; It's my marbled-eyed, red-bottom black-patent angel face in the cute hat." By now Ny and China had approached the table coming from where, I don't know. I nudged Nyla on the arm and said, "Ny, there he is! That's the man; you know the one in the cute hat from Bar French, the one I was telling you guys about? You remember, the one who had me surveying the room looking for him when you all walked in."

China looked up and said, "Who? Oh! You mean the cute, adorable guy that you said had your panties doing the rain dance or something— the one who you were telling us about earlier, right?"

"Yes, you're absolutely correct, and they are dancing right now as we speak; so if you see a puddle in my chair when I stand up, it's just from my Lady Blues being affected by his presence." I slightly pointed my finger in his direction. "There, there he is, standing over there talking to that group of guys." As soon as I said that, he turned around and caught my eyes staring and my finger pointing at him. I can remember at that moment, he immediately cut his conversation short with whoever those guys were, that he was talking to and started walking in my direction. He stared me dead in my face without blinking, with a look of fate and destiny in his eyes; as if he had had an epiphany of me coming there that night and pointing at him at that very instant.

Drake was a class act and I do mean a class *act*! He walked right up to me, sitting at the table with my friends. He stood not even three steps away from me and stared directly in my face for about thirty seconds, only to set his wineglass down on the edge of the bar and then go behind the bar.

He didn't say two words to me. I felt so stupid. I was sure he was coming over to say something to me. I could have passed out and fainted from the surge of heat that filled my body with embarrassment. When he didn't say anything to me, the only thing that was dancing now, was my pride, and it was doing the Running Man, not the Rain Man.

I had to stand up and gain strength. I stood there, just thinking, *what the hell was that about and who the hell does he think he is?* Now that cute confident man I thought he was had turned into an arrogant A-hole. I was so sure he was about to approach me, I had already practiced in my head what I was going to say.

I was a little upset and insulted at this point, yet looking out of my peripheral vision, I could see him going into the registers, pulling money out, and counting it. I just stood there in silence and dismay—that is, until the bells started to go off in my head, like dismissal time in grade school. *What? Is he the owner? Ooh!* Then I thought, *Nah! He couldn't be the owner of this lovely establishment. He ain't all that now! He's probably the manager or something, and he's just trying to front for me, trying to make himself look good by counting down the draws, when he could have waited to do that at the end of the night.*

So I tried to play it off by taking a sip of my drink and fiddling with my purse as if I weren't paying him any attention, but that didn't help my pride because as soon as I looked up, three sets of eyes were looking at me; Nyla's, China's and Diamond's. And they were shouting, "You're so lame and such a dork!"

They were staring at me all weird, looking at me like, "Why didn't you say something?"

I just looked back at them and said, "I don't know why you tricks are looking at me all crazy; he didn't say anything to me, so what was I supposed to do? Tackle the man? I'm still a married woman anyway, and I don't have time for these post-divorce, predating games."

Diamond just looked at me with her sarcastic eyes and said. "Yes, at this moment you are still a married woman, but a married woman who is living in legal separation, who is on the verge of a divorce. So you should have done whatever you thought would work to have caught his attention. Even if that meant knocking that cute-ass hat off his head. Hell, separated married women need love too, and plus, he's the man behind the bar counting the cash. That's what's important! Not Malik with his cheating ass. I bet he isn't running around talking that married crap. He probably at the strip club tossing-dollars to some stripper-ho, as we speak"

Malik and I had been legally separated for over six months by now. Our marriage was on the rocks, floating on thin ice, just minutes away from a drowning divorce. We had been going through major problems, involving infidelity on his behalf. So I decided that separation would be the best way for Malik to figure out what was more important to him:

being a husband and father to his wife and kids, or going out drinking and playing with tramps all night long.

See, in the beginning of my relationship with Malik, we would do all those things together; that was one of the things that attracted me to him. We used to hang together and appreciate each other's company, but once I had Camilla and Malik and I got married, things started to change. Everything started being different. I would be stuck in the house, while Malik would be out enjoying himself; not only that, but starting new relationships, and enjoying the company other women, as well.

The man that Malik had started to become was no longer the man I met years ago. Then after I had Cameron, you know how we women think: well, if I have another baby, maybe he will act right. *Not!* He started acting out even more. The entire time I was pregnant with Cameron, he was in the streets. Hell, my mother had to call him and tell him to get to the hospital 'cause I was in labor; and when he got there, he reeked of Jack Daniels.

This went on for years and years and years; then one day, we had a really bad fight and I said no more. I had to go. I moved out of the house, took the kids, rented a condo, and was legally separated from Malik, pending divorce. So that night I was free, free to mingle without any feelings of guilt in Diamond's eyes. After all, they all knew I was overdue for the attention of a man. And Drake was looking like the number one candidate to bring me up-to-date on what I had been missing.

Nyla turned and whispered, "Don't look now, but he's coming your way. Here's your chance." Right as he was about to walk past, Diamond pushed me right into him. Luckily he was done with his glass of wine that he had just set on the edge of the bar, because that would have been a red mess. I could have killed her. I felt like a sixteen-year-old teenager back in high school who had caught the vapors or something. Now I was even more embarrassed.

He looked up at me with those big marble eyes and that same little smirk grin on his face from earlier. "Excuse me, turquoise-dress, but if you wanted to fight, you should have warned me. Dang, woman, you almost knocked my hat off."

"That was the point!" I heard Diamond mutter under her breath.

"So now I get it," Drake says. "That's why you were over here pointing me out earlier. I was wondering what that was all about. It was because you were picking a fight with me. And to think, I thought it may have been because you were interested in getting to know me, after seeing me at Bar French or something. Well, turquoise-dress, as beautiful and sexy as you are, if a fight is what you desire, you have the wrong guy. I don't fight women, I only love them. And from the looks of things, you need someone to show you how to do more loving and less fighting. How about we take a trip back into my office and see if we can come to some type of agreement on how we can sort this problem out before I have to press charges for assault and call my security?"

I just looked at him like he was crazy, and then he said, "Don't make me call security on you."

For a minute he probably thought I was crazy, because I just stood there looking void and blank faced, like I didn't hear a word he said. Trying to psych myself, I thought, *OK, this confirms that he noticed me at Bar French and has been paying attention to me the whole time and he's also interested in getting to know me better. But do I look like a ho or gold digger to him? I may be a bit overdue sexually, but I'm no ho; and my appearance may say upgraded diva in Beyoncé voice, but I'm no gold digger either. Maybe he got my flirty, promiscuous actions at Bar French twisted with the woman I really am, and that's a lady!*

I looked at him and thought. *He's the one crazy, if he thinks I'm shallow enough to fall for this "Oh, let's go to my office to sort it out" BS*, but the more I stared at him, the more I was like, *Damn, he is sexy and cute as hell. He's actually my type of guy. I might just wanna see what he's talking about. I can always leave if he starts going too far.* I was really trying to psych myself out…*Man, what should I do?*

Then out of nowhere E, spoke to me. E is my alter ego and she's a freak; she's the freak that I never knew existed until I separated from my husband. Eva is the lady I am. Well, E told Eva to let her handle this one and said, *Well, I guess it wouldn't do that much harm if I went back there just for a minute, to hear what he has to say.* But then Eva stepped up and said, *I'm sticking to the fact that I am not a naïve gold-digging ho and I am not about to let him get that move off on me. Huh! Eva is a lady with class and not trash!* Before I could decide whether to go with E or Eva's advice, Drake firmly grabbed my hand. He looked me straight into my eyes, nearly taking my breath away, just with the way he was staring at me—as if he could hear E and Eva debating inside my head and he had decided to listen to E.

Drake had eyes that could read you all over, and he knew exactly what a woman like me needed and wanted; I could see a picture of all my dreams and fantasies in his pupils. I had run across a lot of men that night, but Drake was an exception. He was the only one who dazzled me with his sex appeal as well as his charm. And from the sizzle in my panties, Lady Blues was dazzled too. She was dripping wet with lust, this time doing the salsa in the rain, ready to see what was behind office door number one! Just the confidence Drake displayed by grabbing my hand and that smirky grin he had on his face made Lady Blues feel antsy and overstimulated, with a craving she could not contain. Drake was like cute shoes and good food, and I wanted mine supersized and I needed two pair. I had to have him, if only for one night.

He told my friends I would be right back and lured me into his office. "Right back" went out the window and ending up being closing time.

# 10

## Boss Lady Unleashed

It was a physical attraction of lust just waiting to be unleashed. The things that went on in that back office would have put Jenna Jameson to shame. I felt like a kite floating around in the sky with nothing but a thin string controlling its motion, until gently being struck by a powerful bolt of Drake's lightning. Emotionally confused, but excited about the thought of possibly taking these feelings into my future.

This man had me positioned all over the place: on the table, up against the wall, on the chair; nothing but booty and red bottom stilettos in the air. He had me; all on the fax-copy machine...I think I even sent one or two to somebody. On the floor and any other solid surface that could support us. It was the most over exhilarating, emotional, physical sexual attraction I had ever experienced in my life. Talk about love at first sight; how about sex at first sight? Just thinking about it gives me instant pleasure. I guess you could say that we've been doing what we do now, since day one.

When we finally came up for air, out of sex-intoxication, and came out of that office, the party was over, but ours was just beginning. Drake and I walked out holding hands like a newlywed couple who was still celebrating the honeymoon. Our faces were beaming with pleasure and blushing with embarrassment. Had we really just made out in an office, with someone we had just met about five minutes ago? Had this really just happened?

Then I noticed Nyla and the girls standing up against the wall next to the bathroom, looking as if they had been looking and waiting for me all night, and the pleasure-filled look on my face turned into sexual guilt without the blushing. I was embarrassed, but Drake was still beaming and didn't look too embarrassed anymore. I think he even looked a little cocky. His head lifted, and so did his eyebrows, as to say, "And now what!"

Diamond had to be on a plane in seven hours, but had told Conner that he could leave, and that she would meet him back at his house later. She's so nosy; she wanted to stick around to get the office-room 411, and to give me dirty looks with the rest of them.

I felt like a pink elephant when I saw them looking at me with those "You did not just have sexual relations with that man" looks on their faces. If their looks could kill, I would have been dead the moment I opened that door and stepped out of that office. I read straight through them; I could see all the "Oh no she didn't," "Oh hell no," "You should be ashamed of yourself, you don't even know this man," and all the other criticizing remarks and statements that were circling around in their nosy little heads, just waiting on the perfect time to be released. But, I just smiled at them as if to say, "Whatever. Y'all told me to go for it and I did...and got hooked up!"

Drake took it upon himself to handle the rest; he surprised the heck out of me too.

"I'm sorry; were you ladies waiting on her?" he asked as he fiddled his fingers across my bangs, pushing them back in place. "I apologize for stealing you all's friend, but we had a few things to discuss. Oh! And by the way, ladies, I hate to be the bearer of bad news without having properly met you all yet, but Eva will be going home with me tonight, and if you all are lucky, you'll probably see her tomorrow—that is, if I don't keep her and hold her hostage for the entire weekend." Then he looked at me and asked, "Baby, is that all right with you?" while gently placing my hair behind my ear and staring me directly in the face with those marble magnetic eyes of his, that had turned my eyes into stone immediately.

I answered him by saying, "Whatever you like" in my *Coming to America* voice. "It's all right with me." And then I turned and smiled graciously at all of them.

Boy, you could have bought them all for one penny total, together; Nyla, China, and Diamond were speechless, and so was I. I had no idea he was going to say that. *Is he serious*, I thought, or *is he just gaming on them so I won't look like an embarrassed, hooker?*

Well, sure enough, he was serious. He told Nyla and the girls again that he would be taking me, his girl, home with him, and that if I drove there alone, I would be following behind him; or if they road with me, I could hand them my keys and they could take my car, and drive themselves home. Or better than that, he could get them a car service to take them home and I could leave my car at his club...*his club*, I must add! Yep, it was his.

At that point I think everyone was just outdone, 'cause they all just looked at me and him like we were crazy and said nothing.

"No need to worry, ladies; your friend will be in good hands," he said, handing them all his business card. He told them if they had any questions to feel free to contact him, but only during business hours because tonight he was going to be very busy taking care of something personal, and he did not want to be distracted or disturbed.

They just took the cards, looked at him, then looked back at me and smiled. "E! You better know what you're doing with this one," one of them said, and they walked away.

I told him I had left my car at Bar French and that I had to go get it first.

"You're fine," he said. "I will just call my boy Tony, who owns the place, and tell him to keep an eye on my lady's car. You can just jump in with me and I'll take you to get it later. Oh! And by the way, are you off this weekend? If so, what time do you have to be at work on Monday, 'cause it's a wrap for you unless you have to go to work tomorrow?"

I just looked at him for about a second and then said, "I have absolutely nothing to do. I'm a *boss* just like you; I make my own schedule."

"I like your style, boss. I think we are going to make a cool team. As a matter of fact, that's what I'm going to start calling you...boss lady!"

From the time we stepped into his loft—no, I take that back—from the time we got into his car, the hallway, and on the elevator, it was hands-on. To be truthful, I can't recall a moment when it was hands-off. We were touching and feeling the entire drive there. Hands under dress; hands down panties; hands on breast, booty, and even feet. Yes! You heard me, even feet!

This man told me to take my shoes off and put my feet in his lap while he was driving. He was driving and massaging my feet, kissing, sucking, and licking on toes. If I wasn't done after that office adventure, I was definitely done after the foot-fondling seduction in the car. You could have stuck a fork in me because I was done.

His hands were like magnets on my body. He couldn't keep them off. Hands were all over the place, even hands on hands. I thought the man had transformed into an octopus because hands, arms, elbows, and fingers were everywhere, including on the steering wheel. I couldn't keep up. I was feeling so many hands and fingers on so many different places, at once on my body; I had to look around just to make sure there was no one else in the car with us. Don't let it be a red light—baby, talk about a red-light special! I will never look at stopping at a red light the same way again.

When we finally made it upstairs to his loft from all the time spent on the elevator and in the hallway having foreplay, or should I say twelve-play, once again I was impressed.

His loft was amazing; I could see why his restaurant/club was so soulful and artsy, because his loft was the same way. This was his makeup; this was who he was—contemporary with a retro soul feel, yet soft and intimate. The only difference in Drake's home and The D Spot was the art detail and the intimacy it reflected.

His home had more of a Clay Wright feel to it, and from the dé-cor you could tell he was a bachelor living a bachelor's life. There were no pastel colors, floral prints, or personal photos, just eye-captivating art, a few earth-tone colors, and rugged contemporary furniture. As I walked around looking at and admiring his home, I picked up a broader impression of him. I could tell he was a very organized, conservative, classy, yet stylish and athletic person. He had a lot of suits, shirts, blaz-ers, and ties, which were all on display in his open-wall closet that was all in order by shades of color. He had an open gym area with all sorts of fitness equipment. His furniture was contemporary, yet calm: nothing too overly flamboyant. The counters were earth-tone concrete, and the floor was cement. He was definitely my type of guy. My impression of him became more flattering as I browsed around his place. If there was any-thing I couldn't grasp about him from his way of living and his home, he was showing me in his actions and personality. The only thing that threw me for a loop was a basket of unmated socks in his laundry area. *Hum! I wondered what that was all about. But anyway...*

While I was wandering around his pad, Drake was following me around, lighting candles in every room; he lit about twenty candles throughout his entire loft, filling each room with a cherry-almond, co-conut aroma with a slight hint of vanilla. Then he turned on some old-school soft music, I think it was some LSG or some Gerald Levert or something like that. He poured us two glasses of wine, Manajatwa, and then he sat down on the couch.

"Come and sit down, boss lady," he said in a rather seductive voice. "Come and sit with me."

As I turned around to go sit down on the couch next to him, I thought Gerald had come through the speakers and was talking to me in person. Drake then says, "Relax, boss lady. Just chill. Just lie back, enjoy, and savor the moment and the music." He began to rub his hands across my thighs, and at that very moment, my heart became consumed—consumed with the presence of Drake.

We sat on that couch and talked for about two hours. We talked about everything from politics to music, to what kind of pizza we liked, our hobbies, my kids, my issues, my goals, his goals, his issues. While sitting and talking with him, I felt a sense of comfort and security. Anything negative going on in my life had turned into a positive, instantly. He was what I needed that weekend and just what the doctor ordered, and it has been like that ever since.

Drake was the relief I needed, the relief I had been looking for, for years, ironically found in only one night and in one person. The last statement he said to me that night on that couch was, "I want to taste you!" The way he said, *"Taste you!"* made Lady Blues and my legs quiver. It felt like, he was already tasting me with just those words. I was mentally, physically, and emotionally ready for anything and everything this man wanted to do or taste at that moment.

That night something happened to me that I will never comprehend, and I will forever live in that moment. We made up our own rules of love that night. That was my first trip to ecstasy with Drake; see, what we did in his office was much different from what took place in his loft. This was more passionate, intimate, and quaint. The way our souls collided and connected, I knew that we were meant to be. My heart was writing a love story, and both of our names were in it.

From that moment at his club when he grabbed my hand, he hasn't let it go ever since. You see, Drake and I have already made our connection; therefore, we will never be apart. I have a piece of me in him, and he has a piece of him in me. The way we made our connection from day one, no one and nothing can come in between us. So, I will be OK if the truth is revealed and this mystery woman does have *half on his baby*, because guess what? I have *half on his heart* and in my girl Diamond's voice, "That's what's important!"

I just sit here in this tub, thinking, laughing, and crying; down to my last swallow of wine, and the bottle is now empty as well. The water is nearly cold. Mariah is still spinning, talking about her dream lover and how she needs him to come and rescue her. I'm feeling sad, but a good sad at the same time. It's only about two in the afternoon, and I'm already on nine. My hands and toes are wrinkled, my straight hair has sweated out and has curled up from the steam of the hot water, and I'm just lying here intoxicated and frustrated, all at the same time (*intoxifrustration?*).

I'm trying to drown all the tainted and toxic words I've heard today with positive memories of Drake, a hot bubble bath, candles, music, and wine. Then I realize I need something more powerful than that. So, I begin to pray to God, thinking, *OMG, I must be drunk for real, because hear I go again with this praying stuff. He is not going to take me seriously, considering I'm a drunk and an adulterous; all at the same time. I must be crazy, didn't I already tell myself that God is not going to help me with this situation because it's the devil's playground I'm on.*

But this time, I prayed anyway.

And this time when I start praying, I feel different. I feel connected in my spirit. I don't know if it's the spirit from the wine or what, but I feel something.

*"Dear God, I thank you for everything that you have done for me in my life time. Please forgive me for my sins, even those that I can't remember. I don't want to live selfishly and sinful anymore, and I want to be delivered from the inside out. I love Drake and if you know my heart, then you know I do. My mother and Nyla, always said that you look at the heart of the person, so I know that you know, how I feel about Drake, but I still need to be free, free from this love curse. I cannot believe what I cannot see, and I cannot see what I don't want to believe, so please give me the strength to have an open eye and mind in this situation. Guide me into the right direction and I will follow. I know that Drake is everything; I think I need and want, but I also know that he is not my husband and I am entangled. Please humble my spirit, so I can be honest with myself as well as my fears. I wish I was not in love with him so much and then maybe I would not feel so much pain right now. I wish my feelings could just go back to where they should be, and this is with my husband and pushing to rebuild trust in him, in order to make our relationship better. Let this cup pass from me and place me where I really need to be in your eyes. This has become way more weight than I can carry. Please remove these sandbags of adulterous love from my shoulders and free me of this bondage. In Jesus name, Amen."*

Just as I finish my last sentence of prayer, I hear my cell phone ringing. I jump out of the tub and practically break my neck trying to get to it, feeling the impact of the wine that I just sucked down like a pitcher of Kool-Aid. All the time, I'm thinking, *What if it's Drake, the devil is a lie? What will I say, or should I not say anything at all?* I pick the phone up off the dresser and look at it; body dripping wet and filled with nervousness mixed with tipsiness. *Oh my God! It's Drake! God sure does work fast. Damn! Oops, Lord, I'm sorry I didn't mean to say damn, I meant dang; it's the wine. I apologize.*

"Hello," I say with a nervous and slurring voice.

"Hey, what's up?" he says. "You called me earlier. Where are you and why aren't you at work? I called your office, but I kept getting your assistant, and she kept putting me into your voice mail. I've been in and out of meetings all day, but every time I got a moment, I tried calling you at work. I didn't want to call your cell, because I didn't know who you were around.

"So, when I couldn't get ahold of you at work, I got worried, so I checked my voice mail and got your message, and from the message you left me, you didn't sound too good, which made me even more worried, so I didn't have a choice but to call your cell. You left the message around eleven; where have you been since then? Is everything OK? Why do you sound like you've been drinking? I know you don't drink anymore but you sure sound tipsy. I couldn't even concentrate on what was being said in the meeting from worrying about you. Did that stupid husband of yours do something else stupid to make you upset and have to leave work? Are the kids OK?" he asked all in one breath.

"Oh, I'm fine, and so are the kids; it's nothing," I say. "I had to leave work because Nyla was having some problems, so I left work to meet her. But anyway, Drake, I really need to talk to you. Can you meet me? Are you at home? If so, can I come by? It's really important."

"Well," he says, "I'm not at home right now, and I won't be going home until around four thirty. I have another meeting at three thirty. If you want, you can meet me at the loft around four thirty or five; that will be cool. If I'm not there yet, you know the code to get in the door, right? Not the front door code, but the code to my loft door, I had to change it, and I don't think I gave it to you. It's 3055. What do you need to talk about? Are you sure that everything is OK? I'm only going to ask you one more time, E. Are the kids there or at school? Is Nyla OK? Do you need something? What's going on, and why do you sound like you've been drinking?"

"Drake, everything is OK; stop it! I told you, I am fine. I'll just see you at your house around five. OK, and no, the kids are not here. They are with Malik's mom; now calm down before you go into your meeting."

"OK. I love you Eva."

"I love you too. Bye. I'll see you later." I hang up the phone.

I stood there, body slowly drying from the cold air, yet shivering from chills and nerves. I wonder how he could sound so innocent, as if he is so concerned about my well-being and if everything is OK with me and the kids; knowing he's hiding a kid from me. Or is he? Well, at five I will know one way or the other if what I have heard today is true. Then I'll have to decide and have to ask myself, "What's next?" But, do I even want to know if it's true or not, and will knowing even make a difference? I'm so confused! So I look up to the ceiling and ask God, "Is this you, or is this the trick of the enemy setting me up for failure?" I just shake my head.

I walk back into the bathroom and look at the empty wine bottle. I can't help but think that it's the enemy now, so I get annoyed and instantly grab the bottle and glass, grab my robe, run outside, and toss both the glass and the bottle in the neighbor's trash. I walk back in the house like a tipsy madwoman, now disgusted with myself for even taking a sip of the wine, not to mention knocking off the entire bottle. To add more disgust, I realize I don't even have any shoes on; I done straight walked outside, across the lawn to the alleyway with no shoes on. *That's something that only a drunk would do, I need to really get it together and drink some coffee to help sober me up. Thank God, Malik made some this morning and there's still some left over.* I think.

Now I have to get in the shower to wash my feet and down some coffee; after drinking a whole bottle of wine. I'm going to be sick. Where they do that at? Something is definitely wrong with this picture.

# 11

## Love Affair or Love Unfair

*I* know this meeting with Drake may be a contradiction of my prayers and may even be the trick of the enemy, considering I'd just finished praying to God, asking God to remove me from this emotional love grave that I have somehow buried myself in. I also asked Him to free my life from all the contamination that has infested it during this love affair and to help me return my heart where it needs to be.

So, do I even want to go and meet with Drake? But I need this, I deserve to know the truth; maybe this is my out.

Man, I'm losing it. This man and this situation have me so confused, I don't know if I want to be out or in. So for that reason alone I must go and meet with him, if for nothing else but my sanity and my closure. I must go to see him; I need to see him. I need confirmation of this baby-mama-mess, to free me of my distress and cure me of this love affair gone wrong. For some reason, I can feel it. I can feel it in my gut that everything Nyla told me today is more than the truth and that going to see him is the one thing that will either bring an ending to my sin or open another door to more sin. It's all about choices, and I have to make mine tonight.

With all the tension and stress that I have built up in my mind and body over this situation, my body has become overexerted emotionally, and I can barely focus. Meeting with Drake and hearing what he has to say, is the only thing that will help me better understand and gain some insight on exactly what has transpired, which will help me get a grasp on where I stand, and where this relationship stands, and if it will continue to stand anymore.

Either way, it won't even matter because our relationship was invisible anyway, just like Nyla said. Technically we don't even exist, at least not in the real world. So the only damage control that will need to be done will be to the only two people who know they are involved, and that's Drake and me. Basically I'm just meeting him for closure and/or damage control for us. The more I come to grips with what's about to happen, the more I can come to grips with letting go, if that has to happen, after tonight.

I can barely concentrate on getting dressed without sitting here sifting through memories and life-changing thoughts about what will be said at five o'clock. I feel as though I'm two hours away from another breakdown.

With that being said, what will I be subjected to, after tonight? After he finds out that because he has broken our trust and ruined our setup, I can't deal anymore—that I'm not like him. I can't just go on with my life on a daily basis as if what we have is OK and enough until we have it again; knowing he is making preparations to build a family and a life with another woman. I can't do it. I can't know that he is with someone else, sleeping, eating and sharing intimate moments. Nah, that ain't for me. Kudus to him for doing that for me, but I honestly can't do it! Not only do I feel like I have been betrayed, but I also feel like our arrangement has been betrayed.

But the question, I have to ask myself is, "Do I, as a part-time or shall I say in-between-time lover, even have the right to be upset or to inquire about or question his affairs?" Does the fact that I am a married woman with a whole family of my own give me room to inquire and question his affairs and/or his motives? Should I just be like, "Whatever," and let it go, because technically I don't have a right to do anything else but that?

Am I in violation of the code of conduct we both agreed upon in this relationship? By me questioning him, am I intervening in an area that is totally out of my jurisdiction? And if I was so concerned about Drake and our relationship, why did I move back home to Malik when I say that I have everything I want in Drake? Why didn't I just get the divorce? Was it truly for my children or was that all an excuse for my own selfish benefit, so I would be able to hold on to both my family and my lover all at the same time?

Then, even after I moved back home, Drake still allowed me to have access to him and his home with an open mind. He showed his understanding and compassion for my children, my situation, and my decision. Hell, I have all the codes to this man's home, as if I live there. Well, I did; until he just told me, that he changed the code to his loft door. *Hum! I wonder why he did that and didn't tell me. See, he's doing extra shit already and the baby ain't even here yet!*

I'm in for a lot of changes, I see! *So yeah!* Even though he chooses to have an arrangement and agreement with me and my situation and be understanding about the decision I made about returning home to my family, if this rumor happens to be true about him having a baby on the way by some unknown woman, should I feel obligated to return the favor and act like it's OK? Is it now my turn to be the mature and understanding lover? Will that make our relationship fair and equal?

Those two cups of coffee have truly kicked in, because the tipsiness has turned into hyperness and edginess. With tons of questions bouncing around in my head, unanswered; keeping me confused; steering my heart towards being understanding and considerate to the situation; yet, at the same time; giving me a mixed-emotional breakdown, and making me nervous and unprepared for what's about to be said.

Well, it's do-or-die tonight; whether I'm prepared or not, tonight may be all I have. So, I better lose the nerves and get prepared, 'cause tonight there's going to be a little game of truth or dare going on. Either

I'll hear the truth and accept it, or I will hear a lie and reject it, but I have to hear something, and it has to be from Drake's mouth, *tonight.*

The truth is the only thing that will set me free, but a lie may keep me in bondage; the hard part is being able to recognize what's what, and having the strength to do what's right after the fact, and keeping my emotions out of the equation, so that they don't confuse my judgment.

I have to hear it from him; face to face, not over the phone, not through a text messages, and not from anyone else: that is why I have to go meet him, so I can look into his eyes, the only thing I can always believe in—those big, marble eyes that hold the truth to his soul, that will reveal the answers to all the questions, bouncing around in my head, even if he can't utter a word.

*Yes!* In person, so I can dissect his body language and his eyes. Through his eyes I can see his deepest emotions, and I will know the truth just by the way he looks at me, when he speaks. And his body language; is always a dead giveaway for his emotional state, especially if he is lying.

I probably know this man just as well as I know my husband. So whatever he say or doesn't say, either way I will get the truth out of him—no matter what, even if his mouth won't dare admit to it.

I try pulling myself from my exacerbating thoughts so I can finish getting dressed. *This may be our last encounter,* I think again, *so I have to make myself look extra boss lady fabulous. So let me go get fabulous and get this show on the road.*

I look into the mirror with a little grin and say out loud, "Now turn off that Mariah and stop all that whining; put on some Beyoncé upbeat, diva music and pull it together, like you know how. You know you've been taught by the best. All the crap you have been through with Malik, this should be a breeze. Now get some sexy lingerie out and saturate your body in some smell-good. Grab something sexy but simple to put on. Let's get it together, E, and get this shit over with. Make this last encounter a signature boss move. In Donald Trump's voice, 'Drake, you're fired! Not a blink or a wink! Now take the elevator down; your car is waiting!' Done! Next! If that's what it's going to be!

Or will I be taking the elevator down." *Ha-ha,* I think. *I got to laugh to keep from crying!*"

First I go brush my teeth and drown my mouth in mouthwash, to remove the wine and coffee mixture. Then, I begin caressing my body all over in Drake's favorite refreshing aroma, Frederic Fekkai, which lingers in everything I touch and everything that touches me, before slipping into the Very Sexy Infinity Edge, VS collection, in snazzy black.

The glow of my body from the Frederic Fekkai body cream makes my sugary brown skin resemble honey pouring out of black satin. I slide into my black Prada, peekaboo-toe mules with the five-inch stiletto heel that makes the You Rock-Apulco Red OPI nail polish gleam on my toes like a freshly dipped, red candy apple.

I've oiled my body up, just enough to squeeze into the size twenty-nine, slim-fitted ankle, 7 for All Mankind jeans that got just enough stretch in them to hold on to all the packaging I'm carrying around in the back and just enough rips to show off my sexy thigh cleavage in the front. *Watch out, Kim Kardashian. I hope I don't run into Kanye on the way.*

These sexy low-rise jeans help to accent my Coca-Cola bottle waist that's clinging to a white stretch wife-beater tank top that reads "All Natural No Sugar Needed." My biceps are on full blast, the VS push-up bra has turned the B-cup twins into a C+ and have them pumped up like balloons.

The plan is to seduce Drake by giving him a full screenshot of what he will be missing—his favorite scent that he may never smell anymore but will linger in his aroma Rolodex like it does in his sheets after one of our encounters; his favorite toenail polish that he will never be able to touch to see if it's still wet because of the way it shines, before he kisses each one of my toes, and tells me how he loves that color so much; my boo-tay, that he loves to squeeze like he's shopping for fresh fruit at the Soulard Market, that's sitting firm and tight in the 7's, fitting every angle, like the skin of a delicious apple waiting to be bit; and last but not least, the twins, "his playground of pleasure," which will be looking him directly in his face while he's talking to me, like two luscious melons sitting on ice. That will now be off-limits. *Ohhhh!* Now I'm turned-up and ready. Game on; let's go!

Oh! One more thing; Drake loves my naturally hair, but he loves it even more when it's messy and curls and coils are falling all over my head. Tonight I'm going to pull it up in the back with some sexy hair candy to expose the hair that lies on the nape of my neck like drizzled waves. *That drives him wild!*

So up my hair goes in a sexy two-strand twist in the back, held up by only one black Swarovski crystal pin barrette, with messy curls and coils, falling everywhere in the top. He loves to snatch that pin barrette out when we're making love and then using his hand to hold it up when he's loving me down from the back, *I don't know what that's all about.* Another *sexcapade* thought crosses my mind, and I just smile.

*I need some black bling to match the barrette,* so I'll wear my black diamond hoop earrings and my David Yurman black onyx bracelets with the pave diamonds that Nyla bought me for Christmas. Drake loves it so much; I had to get him the male version of it, for his birthday.

Oh yes, and I'll rock my favorite Michele diamond watch with the stainless band that Drake bought me for my birthday two years ago to take him back down memory lane. That night was a good night; I think I walked around his loft, all night wearing nothing but that watch. That's the same watch that almost got me in trouble with Malik too, because I told him I had purchased it as a gift for myself for my birthday with my Nordstrom bucks and he couldn't imagine me purchasing such an expensive gift for myself with Nordstrom bucks. *Which is so true!* But what was I going to say? "Oh, my lover Drake bought it." LOL! It took me a week of convincing him before he left it alone, and to this day every time I put it on, he looks at me funny and says, "You sure must have spent a lot of money at Nordstrom to have that many bucks for a watch like that."

But all jokes aside, if this is finally the last time for us, I want the sight of me to steal his valor and make him realize he has only cheated himself. When I walk through that Neo-Soul loft of love, before he has the opportunity to bring tears to my eyes and weariness to my dreams by crushing my future with this act of irresponsibility, which may cause us to move in different directions forever, I want him to see that I am his boss lady, the fancy one, the baddest boss chick. *'Cause whoever this other chick is; she ain't me.*

"Oh, that sound good, I may need to tweet that!" I say out loud. Then I just start laughing at myself. *I'm going crazy, this is crazy. How did I let this man get me this entangled to the point where I'm acting like a teenager who just lost her first love to the new girl on the block; engaging in such immature tactics? Doing all this and for what? Because if he was so in love with all this, why am I about to go meet him and discuss another tramp? Man, see where sin will get you!* I just shake my head; thinking, *it will give you bipolar-schizophrenic tendencies!*

It's getting closer and closer to my designated meeting time; five o'clock is rolling around sooner than I thought. I can feel the butterflies starting to swarm around in my stomach, alerting me that it's almost time for me to face my fear.

With all the commotion circling in my mind these last couple of hours, I haven't had time to focus on anything else but Drake and the way I look, so I must have lost track of time. As I stand here looking in the full-length mirror, fixating over my appearance and what's about to happen in less than an hour from now, I realize I haven't spoken with Malik all day, not even this morning before he left for work. The only word I've heard from him was that note he left on my nightstand. Curious.

*Hmm! Why hasn't he called? I wonder what's going on with his behind. I know I forgot to call him, but he hasn't even called the office today because if he had, my assistant would have paged me with the message or put him through to my office voicemail, like she did with Drake. Well, I'm not calling him either. I just hope he doesn't call while I'm with Drake!* I wave my hand as to say forget it. *If he does call, I just won't answer as usual when Drake and I are together. I can't dwell on Malik and what he's up to right now. I have enough on my mind worrying about Drake and his mess. Right now, I have bigger fish to fry and I need to preserve all the energy and sanity I have left for what's about to go down at five with Drake and his new baby mama drama, 'cause I know it true. I can just feel it in my heart.* I squirt one shot of Light Blue and walk into it, do one more mirror check, and head downstairs to the kitchen.

Although I know Malik probably won't be home until late tonight since it's Friday, I'll still leave him a little note on the refrigerator, telling him I'm going to meet some of my coworkers for happy hour and dinner and that I will probably be in a little late tonight. More than likely I'll end up beating Malik home, but just in case he's feeling guilty about our little misunderstanding we had last night and decides not to hang out with those loser buddies or tramps of his all night, and he comes home early, my behind will be covered. You see, I've learned how to play Malik, who tends to think he's playing me; I'm always two steps ahead.

I don't know why, but anytime I tell Malik I'm going out with my co-workers, it gives him a feeling of relief. Maybe he feels like if I'm with my coworkers, it's still slightly considered business, like a business outing or something, and I guess that gives him a sense of security that pacifies his insecurities. I don't know and I don't care, just as long as it works and prevents him from calling and nagging me, getting on my nerves.

You see, he won't make all those stalker calls if he believes I'm with my coworkers because he doesn't want them to be looking at him crazy at the next bring-your-spouse corporate Christmas party like he's some kin to O.J. Simpson; as they whisper to another coworker about how insecure and crazy he be acting.

I finish writing the note and stick it on the refrigerator in clear view so even if he's drunk, he won't miss it. I grab my keys and my Kate Spade Love Birds Wink Clutch and walk toward the garage door. Heading out, I pass the hallway mirror and get a glimpse of myself and think, *Yeah baby. Drake, you done lost a good one!*

# 12

## Dressed Up & in Character

As I pull into the parking lot of Drake's loft, I continue to badger myself with all the so-called excuses I've given him about why I haven't officially left my husband to pursue a real relationship with him. I sit there for a minute, thinking, *If it's left up to me, I will keep wearing my disguise, and he can continue wearing his costume, and we can continue acting out our parts in this romantic love saga and keep pretending that what we have is good for the both of us.*

Why should we have to compromise what we have grown accustomed to, just because of a little bump in the belly? We can't erase our history or the love we share for each other, just because of today. We understand what we have, and it works for us. No one else has to understand us, as long as we do—as long as we understand that the love we share is stronger than just letting go and saying good-bye, over spilt-baby-milk.

Anyway, we both knew going into this what it was and that there is no such thing as a flawless love affair. It should be called a love unfair anyway, because that's the way it's always going to ends up; someone is always going to feel as though they are being cheated or treated unfairly in one way or another. It's an unfair affair, and you have to deal with it, in whatever way it comes if you want to stay in the game.

Right at that moment, my cell phone rings. Before I can draw my attention to my cell phone and pull away from daydreaming about affair statistics in an effort to convince myself to continue this one, I instantly get a rush of anxiety. I look at the time on my dash; it's 5:03 p.m. *Please don't let this be Malik*, I think, even though I know it's not even his ring tone. If this man ever had the worst timing, it would be now. I grab my phone out of the cup holder, look at it with a sting of fear inside me, and then yell out, "Thank you, Jesus!"

God must have been on my side for a brief second, because it was not Malik. It was Drake. I hurried and answered, feeling calm because it wasn't Malik, but hesitant, hoping Drake wasn't calling to say he wasn't at home and/or wouldn't be able to make our meeting.

"Hello," I say.

"Hey," he says. "Where are you? It's five after."

"I'm outside in your parking lot about to buzz myself in."

"Dang," he says. "I thought you were going to call me before you got all the way down here, like you normally do. I've been sitting down here at the LaLa Lounge waiting on you to call, having a few cocktails. I just ordered some sushi, so come down here for a minute right quick, until my order gets done, and wait with me. There's no one in here but me and a few other people; they won't know us. Believe me, you'll be OK. Do you want me to order you a yellowtail roll? I know that's your favorite."

"Yeah, OK, that's fine; I'll be there in about five minutes."

I could barely keep my composure; just the sound of Drake's voice brings joy to my spirit and makes me anxious. No matter what's going on with me, all it takes is the sound of his voice, and I'm good. I love when we have our little outings together because we don't get to have them that often, but every now and then we will get a wild hair up our asses and say fuck it, let's do it. So we will sneak off and have some sushi and a drink or two together. Of course, he'll have sake and I'll have club soda, but we always pick a really intimate secluded place, where we know that no one who knows us will be there to recognize us.

When we are hanging out together like that, it takes our relationship to a whole other level because that's when it starts to feel real. Those are the times that make me want to leave everything and just fly away with him and live happily ever after. It all seems so perfect. We sit as close as we possibly can to each other, like magnets; talking, laughing, playing, feeding each other and eating off each other's plate, looking at each other in awe, as if we've never seen something so beautiful as the sight of us being together enjoying each other's company. Touching, kissing, holding hands, just displaying our love and affection for each other in a public place freely, brings fullness to our relationship and makes us want more.

When we are able to sit back and enjoy the foreplays of life with each other, it is the best feeling we could ever share. It's equivalent to a love story or the movie (*Young at Heart*) from the fifties when Frank Sinatra was the king of romance, and Doris Day was the queen of beauty and class, resembling the lyrics in his song, "The Way We Were"—a pure, natural, romantic, unforgettable love story about a couple of kids in love, appreciating each other. It's something that seems so hard for me to appreciate with my husband, yet seems so natural when it comes to Drake.

I love it when I see people pass us by when we're hanging out together; they always look and stare at us. Sometimes I get nervous thinking they may know us, but then I realize it's not a stare or look of acknowledgment; it's a look of green-eyed, blissful envy, wishing they could have what they believe we possess as a couple, which is visible, true, authentic, unconditional, and everlasting love. They don't know that we're wearing disguises and costumes and that it's all a lie, literally a fairy-tale love story, based on nothing but a make-believe dream.

But they can't see that; they don't recognize us as just two deeply-in-love frauds who share an exclusive love affair that could fatally end our lives. They don't know that we are relationship imposters who are just sitting back and enjoying ourselves, savoring the time and every moment we can spear, trying to make something out of nothing. Living all week through moments like this one, anticipating the next encounter, which may never happen if we aren't careful. All they see is a couple that appears to be deeply in love.

Before I pull up to the valet, I contemplate back and forth in my mind about how I'm going to confront Drake about everything I've heard today. I have to think fast, because the valet guy has spotted me and is heading my way, and I'm starting to get nervous and even more anxious. My mind is starting to close in on me rapidly from all the thinking I've been doing today. My palms are starting to sweat and my body is becoming overheated with anxiety and frustration, indicating it's almost time for show-and-tell.

As the valet opens my door, I ingeniously come to a solution just that quick about how to approach Drake. I decide that I will not discuss the situation until Drake and I are done with our dinner date and have returned back to his loft. Then I will bring it up, but for now I'm not going to cause a scene by bringing it up at LaLa's. I know that there would be a confrontation between us, if I bring it up now, and I am determined not to ruin the moment; after all, this could possibly be our final romantic outing together forever; therefore, I was not bringing any drama to our Sushi Say, "Hasta La Vista" date.

Anyway, the LaLa Lounge is not the place or the time for what is on my mind. If tonight is going to be the end of our romantic road and the dead end to Lovers Lane, I am going to go out like a trooper and a true lady, so I have to turn down the boss lady attitude, for now. I am going to conduct myself as if everything is fine until we get to his loft. Then, if need be, I will become a true lady gone berserk, and the boss lady will rise back up. Until then, I will keep my composure and try to turn a bad situation into a great last date, leaving a lasting impression of maturity and integrity about myself and about our relationship.

After tonight it could be officially over for us, so I intend to sit back and savor every second of this date, appreciating Drake's presence one last time. Instead of turning this date into a final moment for us, I figured I'd flip the script and turn it into a finale moment for us; *Finales are always more exciting than finals. Although they practically mean the same thing, they are viewed differently. Finales always end with an exciting ending, and for some reason people always seem to enjoy them and remember them more. Just think about one of your favorite programs; at the end of the season, the network may say that it's the final episode, but they always promote it as the finale. Finals just end and it's over, but a finale ends with a bang.*

I get out of the truck, looking and smelling amazing; *per the vale guy's compliment,* grab the parking ticket from him, and begin walking toward the restaurant. I can see Drake sitting at a table outside, doing what he does best, living as a free-spirited nature lover, enjoying nature and embracing all it has to offer. Drake loves sitting outside, taking long walks, jogging in the park, and just taking advantage of the free beauty of nature. His love for it has filtered over to me.

He is just sitting there, looking just as fine as he always does, with his Prada mirrored shades on; that show a vivid silhouette reflection of me walking toward him and the table. As he's sitting there, I can tell by the adjustment in his body language that he was taking all of me in, behind those mirrors as I walked toward him.

I am taking him all in as well, sitting there resembling a chocolate John Legend, casually laid-back as usual in a wrinkled T-shirt that bears the question, "Have you seen Aruba lately?" The cut-off sleeves have his perfect biceps on display. His khaki, worn, distressed cargo shorts look to be cut off at the knee, but I know they were made like that, because I was with him when we sneaked into Target together and he bought them. He is wearing neon-yellow Air Max tennis shoes with no socks. *Whooooo,* arms made of steel and legs made to feel.

"Damn, this is my type of guy!" I say to myself, smiling on the inside as I feel a warm tingle from Lady Blues entering my panties. It never fails; this is a natural feeling for her whenever she is in the presence of Drake. As soon as she sees him, she starts to throb and tingle like she's just sitting back relaxing, expecting, and awaiting his entrance. *How could I leave all this, and why would I want to, but why would he betray me like this?*

*Here I go again, with all the questions and confusing thoughts,* I think, as I watch him watch me. He has taken off his shades and is staring at me like he is about to put me on the sushi platter and eat me in whole pieces. I notice him fumbling with his billfold, which is what he does whenever he gets nervous or antsy.

Drake immediately stands as I approach the table, greeting me with a warm and tender smile; he grabs me by my waist, hugging and holding me as tight and as close as his arms and body will allow. He kisses me on the neck while breathing in all of me and my aroma; consuming every scent of me all in one deep breath, including my hair, which he says always smells like Lavender.

He whispers in my ear as he brushes my hair up on the nape of my neck, "Damn, you looking and smelling good as usual. I see you're wearing your birthday gift and our, his-and-her bracelets." Then he goes into acting mode and says in his Denzel voice, "I've been waiting on someone like you all my life."

Then while looking me dead in my face, so close that his nose is touching mine and I can smell the Corona on his breath, he does that little smirky grin he's famous for and kisses me on the nose. He pulls my chair out from opposite his and places it as close to his as he possibly can and asks me to sit with him. I just stand there, Lady Blues melting away in my panties, because this too is also his signature when he's ready for me, and Lady Blues knows it all so well.

It's always like we're seeing each other for the first time, both of us smiling and staring at each other in awe as if we've never seen anything as perfect as us together. It's the perfect scene for a Tyler Perry romance movie.

Drake once told me that the feeling of my body, the scent of my skin, and the texture of my hair gives him an orgasmic identification of who I am—that it sends signals to alert his heart that I'm the only one for him and then keys his mouth to say, "I love you, Eva!" He proclaims that he can smell me even before I arrive, and that is why his eyes always greet mine first.

Not only does Drake claim to know every scent that surfaces through my pores, he also claims he knows every curve to my body, every curl pattern of my hair, every tickle to my toes, along with everything else in between, including my heart and my mind. So in knowing that, I know that he should be able to feel my caution and sense the confusion that's cramming my thoughts as I sit here looking a bit spacey, flipping through the drink menu. I'm trying to hold my composure, just continuing to smile and laugh, acting as if everything is OK and being careful not to give off any red-flag signals that it's not.

I should be good at this because I'm pretending as usual—only this time I'm pretending by myself, pretending that the only secrets Drake and I possess are the ones we have created with each other, not secrets we have separately accumulated on our own.

I just sit here, smiling, laughing, and engaging him with my pretend attention, doing something I never thought I would have to do with him. I'm trying to control my confused angry feelings, and trying to hide my uncertain pain. I'm being extra cautious not to project them through our conversations or my actions before we finish dinner and get back to his loft.

As we sit here eating sushi together, enjoying the atmosphere and the beauty of nature. I'm discreetly watching him, as he's tossing back Coronas and sake, talking and giggling like everything is just peachy in the land of unfair affairs; like he has nothing to hide and no secrets.

I suddenly gaze off into a deep thought, almost a daydream, something that has become a pattern since I met with Nyla this morning and had this ridiculous situation brought to my attention.

I start thinking really hard, so hard that I get lost into a trance and forget I am in Drake's presence. I start thinking about life, thinking about all the distractions that may come across your path on your road to happiness, and how if you feed off those distractions, you will end your journey and never achieve true happiness. Only to realize later, that because you had become so caught up in the distractions, you lost sight on your happiness and now, find yourself turned around, headed back down that road towards misery.

Then all of a sudden, my thoughts redirect themselves into another direction, and my deepest thought becomes my reality. At first it feels a little weird and unpractical for me to be thinking like this, leaving me at a loss to understand my own thinking. But then it begins to make sense, once I begin to analyze my thoughts from a different view and angle, and begin to understand the location of my journey.

I realize that along my road to happiness, I have experienced something very few people have the opportunity to experience. My road may have many distractions, but if I take my time and walk it patiently and wisely, instead of trying to speed past all the signs without reading them, I'll find my way. And my way is the way that leads to love, romance, and happiness, and that's the right way. This is a journey every woman deserves to encounter, and I don't want to have to give it up for anything. Even if it's not legally perfect, it's perfect for me.

Why let distractions detour my journey? If all else fails and this chick is indeed around four months pregnant by Drake, I have at least five months to continue walking this road of happiness and enjoying every step along the way. If he decides this chick is his future and I'm not included, then at that point it will be time for me to take another route or turn back around and go home. But for now I'm not turning back, and I'm going to keep down this road that I enjoy, because this is the only road that makes me appreciate life's journeys, anyway.

I am a woman who has been married for over ten years, and I've yet to feel loved by my husband the way I feel loved by Drake; to experience love at this magnitude is irreplaceable. Therefore I have to put on my poker face, change my point of view, and turn it around to see the light at the end of the tunnel. If indeed Drake has a child on the way and a baby mama to be revealed, I cannot take it personally.

I cannot continue to sweat this situation and let it affect what we have; I have to relax and release. The only thing that should really be bothering me; in all truths, is the fact that Drake has yet to tell me about this situation—that I had to hear it through someone other than him. We should be able to talk about anything, including situations as serious as this one. Drake not discussing this with me makes me feel like I'm being betrayed and cheated out of our trust and loyalty, but not betrayed and cheated in the relationship aspect of it. It's like I've been left in the dark, and why? Why would he hide something like this from me? I'm the closest thing to him, or at least I thought I was. It's not like I have grounds to be upset, when you think about it. After all, how could I let my mind play tricks on me and even consider this as a betrayed relationship or even a cheating one, for that matter, when I'm married?

Just because Drake decided to screw around with another woman, that's not exactly screwing around on me because technically we are not together. I belong to someone else—what do I have to be upset about? I'm more upset about him going in without his raincoat and getting her pregnant, but betrayal and cheating on me...I don't think so; it's more like your bad, Drake, you fucked up! And now you have to deal with it.

Or maybe he didn't fuck up and he wanted this. Maybe he wanted to get involved with someone he could settle down with, have a real family, and a life of his own with. Maybe he's tired of living a pretend life with me. And if he is, how can I be mad at that? Should that really bother me? Or is it just bothering me because of my stubborn, self-centered, selfish, and immature way of thinking? Is that why I feel like he should not be allowed to have those things? Or maybe the reason why I was feeling a little betrayed and cheated is because of my situation at home, because I'm not happy there; when I shouldn't have the nerve, considering my adulterous behavior.

Even the fact that I'm more upset about him not using protection is a gimmick. When I go home to a man every night—my husband, to be exact—at some point I have to be intimate with him. Drake knows this, but yet, Drake has never made moral judgment about me or made me feel like I've betrayed him or cheated on him, so what makes me better or worse than him?

So I have to look at this baby-mama accident chick like this: in my ghetto mentality, *anybody can get fucked, but is anybody really fucking with you?* That's the question that draws a blank; so why should I be mad about Drake screwing some chick, and in his case getting caught, or even about him wanting more of his own life—if indeed that's the case and he is actually *fucking with* this chick like that.

Why should I be upset? Why should I let that upset me and get our situation off balance? This is not something I will have to deal with on a regular basis, just as he doesn't have to deal with my situation on a regular basis; it's all about knowing your place and playing your role. This will be his family and his problem, just as I have my family and my problems. It's not like it's Malik who's having a baby on me. *Now that would be detrimental to everything. That would cause me to file for divorce, take the kids, the house and seek alimony! Straight up!*

Hell, this might work out better for the both of us, after I take it all in. This could make us equal in a sense! After all, why should I spoil everything Drake and I have created over a fuck and a mistake, a fuckin' mistake? Drake has been putting up and dealing with my jacked-up situation for years. It may just be time for me to return the favor. I am a woman with a family and issues, whom Drake just happened to have falling in love with. So even though you try to do the right things, and you try to follow all the rules and guidelines to respect love's territories, you can't always abide by all of them. Especially once feelings get involved. When feelings are as involved as mine and Drake's; when they've become tied to each other like ours have, this makes it even more difficult to try to disconnect and regain control of them.

What Drake and I are about to go through is all a part of the game in a love affair, and if Drake has stood strong and long enough to juggle my life along with his and still stayed in the game without throwing in the towel, it's time for me to stand just as strong and just as long. The tables have turned and the bottle has stopped spinning, and this time it's stopped right in front of me. It's my turn, it's all a part of being in the game; you can't be in it and not play when it's your turn. I just hope the game doesn't change its direction and leave me playing alone.

Therefore, I will approach Drake with understanding and address my concerns in a reasonable way, being careful not to react negatively so that he in turn will act the same. Although I know that Drake has always been upfront and truthful with me in the past and that he would never intentionally lie to me or hurt me on purpose, in a situation like this, you never know what the outcome may be or what might be said. Although I think I want to know the truth, sometimes the truth can be more than a person can handle; especially when it's a baby involved.

See, when you're entangled and enjoying the moment, it's all good. But when the tables are turned and the rabbit gets the gun. Then it can go all bad. It's the aftereffect of the love affair that could be detrimental. So I have to stay focused and get my mind right, if I'm going to be about this life.

# 13

## Keep Juggling or Drop the Balls

"Eva, Eva, Eva!" Drake says. "Are you OK? I have called your name over five times already, and you haven't blinked or said a word."

When I finally hear Drake calling my name, I snap clean out of my daydream and realize that he is looking me dead in my face, like I'm a crazy person and I've taken some drugs or something. He's all confused at why I didn't hear him, when I'm sitting, not even two inches away from him.

"What's going on in that pretty little head of yours? You didn't hear me calling you all those times and you're sitting right next to me. Girl, you had me scared for a minute, I was about to start shaking you, really hard! But you've been acting real funny ever since I spoke to you on the phone earlier today; you was sounding all drunk, number one, and number two you been sipping on my sake and to my understanding you don't drink anymore, right? I guess you thought I didn't notice. You haven't picked up a drink in over three years E, ever since your sister totaled your car a few years ago, drinking and driving. So something's going on with you, and I know it, 'cause I know you.

"You haven't even touched your yellowtail roll that you love so much, yet you been drinking my sake and daydreaming for about ten minutes, acting like you on something. Are you on something? It sure isn't the sake, 'cause it don't do much of anything unless you sipping something else with it. So are you going to tell me what's on your mind and what's going on, or what?

"Not only that, but I almost forgot you called me talking about you needed to meet with me. Man, girl, you and all that sexiness has thrown me all off. I almost forgot about that. You called me and left me a message; you said you needed to talk to me, and it sounded urgent, so now I really want to know what's up. What did you need to meet with me about? Did you finally file for divorce or something? Oh, is that why you have been drinking? You celebrating? Well, tell me so I can celebrate with you!"

He does that famous smirky grin he always does but this time he was serious.

I smile and say, "Ha-ha, very funny." Under my breath I mutter, "Oh, so you worried about me getting a divorce? What life-changing event are you about to celebrate? You tell me what's up."

"What?" he says with a mouth full of sushi. His eyes open up as wide as double doors, but I know he doesn't hear me, because I say it so softly that I can barely hear myself; I just smile.

"Oh nothing, I was just saying that this sake sure tastes good. It's been a long time since I had some. But you're right; I probably should stop drinking before it gets me in trouble."

"E, don't play with me. I know that's not what you said, but if you don't want to talk to me and tell me what's really going on, that's fine. But you know whatever it is, I'm here for you. You know you can talk to me about anything. If you tell me, I bet I can make whatever it is all better. You're my girl, E: my lady, my chick, my love, my best friend! Girl, you know I'll do anything for your sexy ass. Gone hop out that truck on me like that today, walking toward me looking all supple and sexy, smelling all good—girl, I was like, damn, I love that girl right there... She gettin' it tonight!"

I look into those marble eyes of his, exhale slowly, smile, and say, "I love you too, Drake; I love you too."

He gently places a piece of his sushi in my mouth and says, "Eat something," then whispers, "Whatever you need, whatever you want, or whatever I can do to make it better, I will. Whatever you're going through, I got you. You must have forgotten that we are in this together, no matter what happens or what doesn't happen. I'm not going anywhere and I hope that you aren't either, but you cannot hold back on me and keep me out of the loop. You left work early today; I was just with you yesterday, E. If you were planning on leaving work early, you would have told me yesterday; then the staring off into space in deep thought, to the point that you didn't even hear me calling your name all those times, and you sitting right next to me. I'm not even going to bring up the drinking anymore 'cause you already know that's a red flag. Plus, you distinctively stated when you called me that you needed to meet with me, to talk to me.

"E, I don't know if you know this or not, but if you don't, I'm going to let you know, girl, I know you like I know me. I know you better than you think. I know that when you want to see me, you just call me and say, 'I want to see you, now!' Or 'Meet me, now!' Or 'I need you, now!' Never do you say; I really need to meet with you. That sounds like I'm about to get fired or I've fucked something up and you need to check me or something, but I'm not one of your employees and I would never do anything out of order to you, so that couldn't be it.

"You have to let me in, Eva, and you have to communicate with me and convey to me what's bothering you or what's on your mind or what you're going through. That's the only way I can help. I know you all independent and you a boss and you don't need nobody to help you 'cause you got it all figured out in your ghetto diva voice. But, E, everybody needs somebody sometimes, and I'm not just fucking you. I'm not just your fuck buddy. *I fucking with you, it's like that; we are together.* I have responsibilities in this relationship too, even though I know you have what you have going on at home, and it may sound crazy to some people but not to me: I'm still your man and I have to be accountable for you too.

"It is what it is. I sleep with you more than he does, so my responsibility should be greater. Our situation doesn't intimidate me. It makes me want to stand up even more, so you'll know what you have in me and you'll know that whatever happens or doesn't happen, I got you. I'm here for you whenever you decide and whatever you decide.

"For now I'm going to shut up and leave it alone before I start to get all in my feelings, *as you say,* but you get the picture. Now, we are going to go on enjoying the rest of our evening, at least until your cell starts ringing off the hook and you have to jump up, leave me, and go home to that dude." He gives me another smirk smile as he leans over and gives me a peck on the cheek.

I just look at him and say, "Now with all that you just said, why would you have to go there at the end? You always trying to get something off. Eat your sushi and shut up and don't worry about the small fish, I got that handled; you got bigger fish to fry, honey! And by the way, you had me at the first *I love you.*"

He laughs. "You so ghetto, but so cute; don't be rolling your neck at me like that, and fix your face. I know I had you at *I love you*; I just wanted to confirm how much." He kisses me on the lips and pinches my right cheek. "I love me some you, girl; I love my fancy ghetto boss chick! Let's go!"

He beckons for the waiter to bring the check and starts to look at me with the eyes of lust, as if to say it's about to go down as soon as I get you up those stairs and in that loft. My Lady Blues is yelling, "*Yeeeeaaasss! It's about time!*"

He pulls my seat out and grabs me by the hand, clutching it between his fists. I gaze up at him and damn near lose it. I can't believe it. I came all the way down here to talk to him about these rumors about him getting some chick pregnant. I been going through hell all day, fighting with my emotions and my mind about how I was going to confront him about this dumb shit, and now I'm falling back in his web; it's the overlay for the underplay. He done flipped the script on my ass, just like I did on Malik's ass last night, but he used the good-guy tactic on me. I feel like I've been flipped.

Lady Blues dries up instantly just from that thought. Now, I am not in the mood; Lady Blues is dry and I'm upset again.

I've been sitting here thinking, looking all spaced-out, damn near dumbfounded like a daydreaming weirdo, trying to rationalize this crap and make it fall in the best interest of both of us. Then he goes and uses this lame-ass tactic of concern and empathy towards me and what he thinks I'm going through, in an effort to make himself look like the good guy. *E, I love you, I'm here for you. Whatever you need, I got you. It's us all day, baby, we together. Let me in; I'm responsible for you!*

Everything he just said while we were sitting down has just crossed my mind, but what I don't remember is how mushy I felt when I heard it. Because, I am now upset again.

I start venting to myself in my head. *He would not have the nerve to say all this shit to me right now, when he's the one who won't let me in.* Then I look at the way he is clenching and gripping my hand as if he is trying to hold on for dear life 'cause he's scared I am going to run off. I gaze into those big marble eyes of his, thinking to myself as we stand waiting for the valet to bring our cars around, *I am not going to snap and go bananas right now; I'm going to hold it all in until we get back to his loft.* He thinks he's about to get laid. Yeah, he's about to get laid all right—laid the fuck out, if he don't lay it all out and tell me the truth. Yeah, he always calling me ghetto on the slide, but I really should show him ghetto right now and just start yelling out loud, loud as I possibly can, *What the hell were you thinking, fucking up our plans like this? Or were you even thinking at all?* But I have to stay calm and revert back to my character from moments ago and continue to pretend that everything is OK. *I'm telling you, this bipolar crap is real! It will sneak up on you when you least expect it.* I thought.

Man, I am so mad, that my throat feels like it is about to cave in and collapse from holding back all the tears and frustration I am feeling. I put my shades on; because I know that my eyes are turning red from holding back the tears and the angry frustration. By now I am like, where is that damn valet man with my car? He ain't getting a tip. This date is officially over and I'm ready to go.

Now, I don't even know if I want to go with him back to his loft. I'm so upset, I just want to sit in my car and cry all the pain away, but I know I have to hear what he has to say about the BS. So, I know I have to go back with him, if just for that reason.

*I can't believe he just sat here like we have no worries and he's playing his part of being the best man ever*, I think and shake my head.

Now I am feeling anxious. I see my truck pulling around. I am ready to get everything I have to get off my chest. It is about to be show time. I am hyped. I get in my truck, don't give the valet a tip at all, but then I see Drake hand him a five and I'm like, *OK, so he still trying to play Mr. Perfect. Ohhhhh! This is working my nerves and it's starting to get annoying.* I just sit there for another two minutes in my truck until I see Drake's car pull around and that makes me even more upset, 'cause he jumps in his 650, looking all Hollywood, with his shades back on and the top down.

"Oh, so now he's Mr. Perfect and Mr. Hollywood!" I say. "He makes me sick!"

Then all of a sudden my cell rings; once again I start to panic, thinking it has to be Malik for real this time. But luckily, again it wasn't; instead, it was Drake. I just look at the phone and say, "Now what, dammit?"

I let it ring a few times to collect myself and get back in character and then I answer. "Hey, babe, what's up? You miss me already? You just left me."

"Yeah, you know I miss you. You should be in the car with me anyway, enjoying this nice day with the top down, your curls blowing all in the wind. But since I know that can't happen, not in the Lou anyway, I just wanted to make sure you were OK and also, make sure that you were still going to follow me home."

I say in my sarcastic voice, "Oh, that's so sweet. I would love to be riding shot-gun with you on a day like today, and yes, I'm okay and you know I'm right behind you. I would never veer off. You can trust that."

He just laughs. "OK, I'm about to pull off. See you in a minute, crazy."

"OK, right behind you, luv!" When I end the call, I'm like, *Man, this dude lucky I love him the way I do 'cause this shit would be a wrap, all this sneaking and following and acting. I'm ready to get to the bottom of it all. I'm ready to lay all my questions out, so I hope he's ready to answer them. I just want it to be over. All the unanswered questions are killing me; all the uncertain thoughts are driving me nuts. Everything about this entire situation has me going crazy; I need closure. I'm ready to be relieved from the state of not knowing, regardless of what the outcome is.*

*So what,* if he has another woman in his life and a baby on the way? *So what,* if everything doesn't go the way I would hope and questions go unanswered. *So what! So what!*

This is all replaying in my mind over and over again as I follow behind Drake. I look at him driving in front of me, and I notice that he had taken his shades off. Those big, marble eyes of his are staring right at me through his rearview mirror, as if to say, *don't leave me. I'm going to make it right. Just continue to follow me. Please don't turn away and leave me on this road all alone. I need you.*

I just smile at him as he looks back at me through his rearview; all I can think about is how Drake and I have had such a ball together these past few years, and how Drake is the blood that keeps my heart pumping regularly. Now why would I want to stop that from flowing? And how lucky am I to have found such a man.

If any woman has experienced loving a man the way I love Drake, they will agree with me when I say, I have to be honest and reasonable with myself about my feelings—not only about this situation, but also about my feelings and involvement in this situation. And that's real talk!

If I can't be honest and reasonable with myself, how do I expect Drake to be honest and reasonable with me and with his self? In all honesty, I don't want to drop the ball. I want to keep juggling regardless of the consequences because it feels good, not only to me but also to him. Heck, he just spilled all the beans, regarding his feelings for me today, so I know it feels good to him.

I do believe that Drake and I have formed such a strong bound, that no one and nothing can come in-between it, not even a baby or a baby mama, because our hearts and the love we have for each other will be the magnetic force that holds us together. If for some reason tonight does kill us, then it was just not meant to be, and that means that Drake is not only Mr. Perfect and Mr. Hollywood, but he is also Mr. Pretender, too. Because that would mean we had nothing, and our love was all a lie, not just to the world, but to us.

In the midst of my thoughts; I hear a murmur on the radio that sounds like Beyoncé. I love me some Beyoncé and she can always lift my spirits, so I turn it up, and when I do, I hear the voice even more clear. Beyoncé is singing "I'd Rather Go Blind," the Etta James song she remade off the *Cadillac Records* film. That song hit me like a bolt of lightning sent in the form of a bow and arrow from Cupid. *Something told me it was over!* That's the first thing that rang in my ears. *I would rather go blind than see you walk away from me! I was just sitting here thinking about your kisses and warm embrace.*

I have never really listened to the words of that song in such depth until today. At this moment while still following Drake I listen. I hear and understand every word, and my feelings for Drake rise up for battle, like a soldier, and says, "Eva, you love him, you know you love him, and there's nothing you can do about it. You can't control it, so I don't even know why you're trying, but if you love him, if you really love him, you're going to have to get a divorce. You're going to have to take your kids, and this time, don't turn back; but that's only if you love him and if you want to be happy. Your kids will understand. They know what's going on with you and Malik. They are not babies anymore, and they want you to be happy. The only issue now, is that it's going to be an added addition, and you're going to have to be understanding with everything, just as he was with you. If he tells you the truth and is honest with you tonight, then get a divorce and marry this man, if that's what he desires. Don't miss out on the love of your life and substitute love for convenience, for the rest of your life. Malik is convenient; but you are in love with Drake Grimley."

Then I hear Beyoncé say, *"I love you so much that I don't want to watch you leave me, baby; but most of all I just don't, I just don't want to be free."*

We make it to Drake's loft and are just pulling into the lot when all of a sudden my phone starts to ring. This time I am sure it has to be Malik, but with the mood I am in from listening to B, I really don't care. I pick up the phone and say hello in this "don't fuck with me right now, 'cause it's about to be over and you don't even understand" voice. Then I hear a woman's voice on the other end. It doesn't sound familiar at first, and then I realize it's China.

"China, is this you? Girl, stop playing on my phone, and what's up? I'm about to walk into Target." I'm trying to hurry and get her off the phone before Drake gets out of his car and walks over to mine. I have a few extra seconds to spare because I know he has to put the top up, but I really don't want to talk to her anyway.

"Girl, ain't nobody playing on your phone; I'm in the studio with my friend, and my voice is echoing 'cause he has a recording session going on right now. I was calling you to see if you had spoken with Nyla today." I just looked at the phone, like, *Bitch, you my girl, but you know I spoke with Nyla today. Hell, you the one who set it up for real. You just calling to see how I'm holding up because you nosy but you scared to ask, so you beating around the bush.*

"Yeah, I talk to her, why China?" Then I go off. "And why you act like you afraid to come to me and tell me shit? You knew Drake was fucking around and had a bitch pregnant and you called Nyla and told her before you told me. What type of shit is that? You and me are just as close as me and Nyla...Why you call her? This shit is about me, not about her..."

I just keep on going until I hear her yell, "Shut the fuck up! I'm already looking stupid, and I didn't want to call you now, but when I called Nyla and asked her to call you, she told me she was done with me in regards to this situation, and that I had to make my own call. So I'm calling your mean ass on my own. But since you must know why I didn't call you and tell you. It's because you are mean. You are a mean-ass unhappy bitch. The only time you're half-way happy is when you are with Drake; he is the only thing that makes you the Eva I used to know. I don't understand why you just don't leave that ungrateful drunk, cheating, staying-out-all-night-ass Malik for good and take your kids and marry Drake and be happy for the rest of your life, if that's what you really want."

"What the hell is your problem?" I ask, with an attitude. "You know what, you are probably right. I am angry a lot, and that's because I've gotten myself into a mess that I can't get out of, and it bothers me every day. I sometimes wish I were more like you, single and free to go and do whatever I want, and just live my life, being happy and free whether it's hanging out at a studio or with my kids or with my girls, or with the man I really love. But now, that's all fucked up too, 'cause he's about to have a baby by some tramp.

"China!" I say with weakness in my voice. "A whole baby, and not only that; another woman: a chick that he is going to have to deal with, for the rest of his life or at least eighteen to twenty years of it. I'm tired, China, I'm really tired. I just want to be happy, and now I don't know if it will ever happen for me." Tears roll down my face and I'm crying like Drake is not almost done putting his top up and about to walk over to my car at any minute.

I realize China is crying too. "Don't cry for me," I say. "I made this mess, so now I have to fix it, which is what I'm about to do. I'm not at Target. I'm about to walk into Drake's loft and confront him, not knowing if he's going to reject me or what. China, when I say I'm confused, I mean a part of me wants to say fuck it and deal with it 'cause I love him so much. But then, I feel like I would only be hurting him and me. Can you believe I'm even concerned about the chick and the kid? I'm all fucked up."

"E, I'm sorry," China says. "I'm so sorry. Stop crying. I don't know how to tell you, but I'm just going to say it. Sometimes I can be so nosy that I can misconstrue shit. When it comes to my girls, it's like I'm a bull and I see all red when I hear something. But this time I heard wrong; it wasn't Drake who Ellis was talking about. I thought he said Drake's name, but then today, when I came to the studio, the girl was here, and I couldn't understand why she was all over this guy named Drano. So I say to Ellis, I thought you said her baby daddy name was Drake. And he said it is Dre. That's what we call Drano: Dre for short. I said so you're saying *Dre*, not *Drake*, and he said yes: *Dre*, not *Drake*, as in Drake the rapper. It's Dre, as in Dr. Dre. So, with that said, it's not Drake, it's not Drake. That's your man. He loves you and you love him, so go get him. Get off this phone and go get your man."

I can't believe what I just heard. This has me in a state of shock, and now the tears are really coming down. I just can't believe it; everything about today is replaying in my head like a speeding bullet. Then I see Drake, walking towards my truck from a far. I looked at the dash, and it reads seven fifteen. I tell China I love her and that I will call her back and end the call. I quickly call my boy Larry, who has been in my life forever 'cause we grew up in the hood together. He went off to school and came back an attorney. He picks up immediately.

"What's up, E? It's seven fifteen on a Friday night. Did Malik get drunk already and crash another one of your cars?"

"You are real funny, but no, that's not it this time. And don't say that over the phone, you don't know who could be listening in. You know everyone thinks that my sister crashed my car. I never should have let her take the blame for Malik's ass, but that's me; the cleaner, trying to keep him from going to jail and losing his broker's license over another DWI.

That said, I need you to file those papers; you know the ones I've been talking about for years. And get them sent to his job. Hello? Hello?" I say.

"Not a problem," Larry says. "I have been waiting on this call for years. That dude probably deserved you when you were twenty, but not now; and he doesn't deserve those kids. As a matter of fact, I'm going into the office and I'm going to do that in the morning, on a Saturday, so he will get the papers on Monday morning. Hey, E, I'm proud of you. I know it's not my place to say, but I think you're making the right decision, as long as you're doing it for all the right reasons.

It's time for you to free yourself from all that mess, 'cause I don't want another one in the morning call about that alcoholic. The only reason I was looking out for him, was for you, anyway; so I got you. I'll call you tomorrow with the specifics!"

He hangs up right when Drake is opening my door.

"Babe, you saw me over there struggling with that top," he says. "Why you didn't get out and help? You all in here on the phone yapping. I hope that wasn't that ol' drunk-ass dude calling pestering you; I'm sorry, I take that back. I don't want to be disrespectful, that's why I was trying to give you a minute, to finish your conversation, before walking over here. *And are you crying?*

"No, that wasn't him. It's Friday night; you know I haven't talked to him all day. You know how my Fridays go. I'm glad I won't have to put up with that mess anymore after Monday."

Drake helps me out of my truck and closes my door behind me. "What did you say?"

"You heard me; I said; I won't have to put up with that mess anymore after Monday." Drake just looks at me crazy, like he saw a ghost. As he presses the code to get in the front door of his building, and gives me a light smile.

"What's going on Monday? What does Monday have to do with anything?"

Without any hesitation; I just blurt it out. "That was Larry I was talking to on the phone...you know, my friend who's an attorney. This coming Monday is the day that Larry will be serving Malik with divorce papers. So, *Yes!* I've been crying; crying tears of joy! This weekend is the beginning of my new life. I need to find me a three-bedroom condo or a loft or something so I can get started moving as soon as possible. And by the way. I have a few more confessions. I say. As we step into the elevator.

"Remember when I told you that one of my sisters, had an accident in my car, and totaled it out while drinking and driving? Well, I lied; it was Malik. He is an alcoholic and he has been one for years. Of course you know that, but what you didn't know is that he was coming from some strip club in Illinois with some half-dressed stripper in the car—*my car*—with him at the time of the accident. The last time I left him; that was the reason, among a lot of other things. But because he had always been there for me, when I was younger and was the only man I could depend on in life; since I really never knew my father or had a man in my life, I always excused what he did and went back. I felt like I owed him something for paying my way through college and saving me from the ghetto, when in reality; I saved myself, he just paid for it.

"Yeah, it may have been a little bit about my kids, but most of it was out of obligation. I felt like it was my obligation to stick with him even though it was killing me. Plus, I was afraid to leave that lifestyle. He needed me to keep up appearance as much as I wanted to, out of pride—to make everyone think we had the perfect marriage and the perfect life. You know the fairy tale of marrying your first lover and having the two perfect kids, a girl and a boy, along with the perfect careers with the perfect house on the perfect block. Well, yeah, that's what it was all about, until today.

"Then today it became something different. Today I realized that when you really love someone, and I mean truly love someone, it's not based on what they can do for you. It's based on something that comes from a place deep down inside of you; something that's more powerful. That the thought of being without that person will drive you insane because you know that person completes you in every way possible, and makes you the happiest you've ever been in your entire life, other than the birth of your children.

"And even if there were no house, no cars, no careers, and no money, you would still be happy. Therefore, I had to make a decision to choose what means the most to me.

"Is keeping up the appearance of being happy, while living in misery, more important than living with the man of your dreams and actually being happy, is what I had to ask myself?

"Well, after asking myself that question; along with today's string of events, I made my choice, and I choose to let go of the misery! I choose love and happiness! I choose you! And one day when we are married and laying in the bed after doing what we are about do in a few minutes, once we get off this elevator and walk into my comfortable place, I'll tell you all about, the string of events and how crazy this day has been for me, for real. *You have no idea!*

"But for now all I have to tell you is, I choose to be happy, and I don't care about keeping up any more appearances. I'm done acting. I'm hanging up my disguise and I'm choosing you! I love you, Drake Grimley, and one day here soon, I hope to wake up next to the man of my dreams and hear him say, 'Good morning, Mrs. Grimley!'"

Drake instantly pushes the emergency brake on the elevator and takes me in his arms.

"Will you marry me, Eva?" he asks. Then he laughs and does his famous little smirky grin. "You know, I mean after all this is over and you're finally free—divorced—and available to be Mrs. Grimley."

I just look at those big, marble eyes that I fell in love with years ago. "I wouldn't expect to have it any other way." Then I kiss him as if we are already standing at the altar."

That night on the elevator is just like our first encounter; we make love till the cops come knocking. And I mean literally come knocking, because we both forgot he had stopped the elevator, and the silent alarm had alerted the fire department and the police.

When we get off the elevator twenty minutes later, the lobby is packed with women and men all dressed in uniforms ready to save us. What they don't know, is that we have already saved ourselves.

Drake grabs me by the hand and says to the firefighters and the policeman, "Oh, it's all good. We will be OK. The elevator just stopped mid-floor. We'll just take the stairs from here." I just look at him and laugh, and we both run up the back stairs that I know, *oh* so well. Before we can get through his loft door, we are back at it again. Once again Lady Blues is hitting notes like she is Alicia Keys: on the floor, on the couch, in the tub...I don't even remember when we made it past those frosted doors to the bedroom, but y'all know the story. You know how we do what we do, when we do.

That Monday Malik is served with papers, but not at work. He is served in jail because that Friday night he got locked up again for drunk driving. This time, he didn't have me to sneak him out of the car and act as if my sister Rolando was the stripper driving, that had run off and left my car; sitting-totaled. Nor, did he have Larry to get him out of jail with all his connections.

Oh, and yeah you heard me; the stripper who was in the car with Malik, jumped out and took off running when Malik got into the accident, that totaled my car. So, me being the obligated wife, I call up my baby-making-sister Rolando, and gave her $1,000 to take the blame.

And asked her to act like she was the stripper driving that jumped out, and ran off. Plus I had to pay Larry to handle the case. All in an effort to save Malik's behind, so that he wouldn't get in more trouble and lose his broker's license. The judge had already given him a warning, stating that any more DWI incidents would result in him serving jail time and losing his license: immediately because he had previously been arrested on DWI charges a few months prior. So I felt obligated to save him, once again; even though I knew that he was with another woman, when he had the accident in my car.

Well, because of the incident prior, and now this one, Larry asks the judge to make Malik move out of the house until the divorce is final, so the kids won't be inconvenienced during the school season. Malik has no problem with it because his alcoholism has haunted him and this time he did get in trouble. He has to do ninety day in the pen. He loses his broker's license and can't get it back until he finishes a course for substance abuse-traffic offenders, and completes one year of AA, and he still can't get his license back until his two-year suspension is up. Then he has to take the broker's test all over again.

So Malik ends up moving out and moving in with that same hooker, who ran and left him when he totaled my car; who by the way is only twenty-five-years-old and a stripper. *Still!*

I find out that he has been messing with this chick and cheating on me for years. Yeah, Larry puts his wife, a private investigator, on the case, and she digs it all up. That being said, Larry goes in on Malik, and in the end I get full custody of the kids, plus the house.

Now, six months later, Drake and I are engaged and planning our wedding. We set two different dates, June second or the fourth of next year, because his birthday is on the second and mine is on the fourth.

For now it's all up in the air; but we are even thinking about having it on the twelfth to be able to share our new union with my BFF Nyla and her husband Jamal, and the renewal of their union. If Jamal can introduce me to Nyla and we become best friends, it may just work for Drake and Jamal. Truth be told, Jamal and Drake been hanging kind of heavy, since he and I both have giving our life to Christ. Heck, Drake has stopped drinking and is teaching Sunday school at Nyla's father's church now.

Drake and I are looking to buy a new home in a more historical neighborhood that's closer to everything we like to do, so that he, the kids, and I can either walk or ride our bikes and not always have to drive everywhere, since we all love the outdoors so much. The kids are now going to a private school in the city, and they love it.

Thank God, the kids adore Drake and are happy for me. I think it was China who told me that they knew I was unhappy with their father. That's one story she got right, because when I sat them down and talked to them about Malik and I, they already knew what was going on. They say they were just waiting on us to have the talk. Then when I introduced them to Drake, it was like he has known them forever, and they just hit it off, right off the bat.

They still love their dad, and that I never want to change. Every Sunday when Drake opens up in prayer before Sunday school starts, at the end, I see Cameron and Camilla holding hands, and then I hear Camilla say, "And give a special blessing to my father." It brings joy to my heart, because that means that all those years we were together weren't all a waste.

They get to spend time with their dad every other weekend, and they appreciate that he's honestly trying to get help for his drinking addiction; since it has caused him to lose everything. And to be honest, they even like his girlfriend (the stripper) and their new baby sister Dynasty, who is right around seven months old now. So that means the stripper was pregnant before I filed for divorce. How about those apples?

Camilla always say, "Dynasty is my little sister and all, and I love her, but don't you think Dad was a little too old to be having another baby, and don't you think that was really quick, and don't you think his girlfriend, is a little too young for him?"

I just laugh and tell Camilla, "Honey, sometimes God does things with a twist, to give people a second chance."

I also tell Camilla not to be over there learning any weird dance moves or playing on any poles. Then, I'll tell Cameron not to take any single dollar bills with him, when he goes over there. It's my little joke, but they don't get it.

Oh, and Nyla is still being Nyla. She's still holding on to China's misunderstanding about the whole baby-mama thing with Drake and will bring it up every time China tries to tell a story. It's too funny, 'cause Nyla will be like, "Now, China; is this the real story or is this your story? Is it Dre or Drake?" I just laugh and shake my head.

But all in all, Nyla is happy that I've finally put an end to the drama and made a decision. She's happy about the decision I made, both personally and spiritually. Especially since we've all dedicated our lives to Christ as a family, and now attends her dad's church.

Drake said something so powerful to me, and it really opened my eyes, spiritually. He said that, he felt as a family, we needed something stronger than just our love. After I told him all the stories about me and Malik, he was like, no way that is happening to us; we got to make this right. Those kids can't see another failed marriage or even a dysfunctional home, for that matter, and the only way that's not going to happen, is if we put God into the equation—someone that's going to hold both of us accountable for our actions and keep us grounded, so that we can teach, and show our kids, what real love looks like.

See, that's one of the things I didn't have with Malik; he never went to church or read the Word of God, so I didn't. The only time I was around the Word was when I was around Nyla or Jamal. It's crazy, because I grew up on the Word; was around the church, all my life. Met Malik and fell completely off. I got so caught up on everything else, and lost focus on what was really important.

When Drake said, what he said to me; it took me back to my mother; before she died; she would always say to me. Malik's a good provider; but if you and my grandbabies are going to make it, in this world. You need more than a provider. You need a Provider, a Protector and a Priest and that's what I have now, in Drake.

So, yeah! Nyla is really, liking on Drake more and more, I think she may even love him. I've noticed that she's been calling him brother in-law here lately. I think she may have had a touch of deja vu.

Nyla still keeps up with what's going on with Malik because of Jamal, and every now and then she'll mention, how well she's heard he is doing, in his AA meetings, and that she's so glad he is finally getting help for his alcoholism disease; she even says that this last accident may have forced him to help himself and that me leaving him may have somehow saved his life, even though he has to start from scratch.

You know she's always been the analytical and spiritual one. Remember, she's the smart sister I never had.

China is still dating Ellis; I think he may be the one. If not it won't matter, 'cause she will just keep it moving anyway, but at least I finally got a chance to meet him.

Diamond Nosy Behind is thinking about moving back to St. Louis because after what happened with China and her misinterpretation about Drake, Diamond was like, y'all need me there; I'm a doctor. I heal people and y'all all need healing, and I can get a job anywhere. Plus, my man lives there. I'm coming home before the weddings.

I mean, this girl was calling long distance from her doctor's office, trying to get the 411, and she is still trying to catch up on all that happened that Friday when I filed for divorce. Just *nosy*!

So basically, I'm happy, the kids are happy, my girls are happy because I'm happy, Drake's hella happy—hell, he gets to get this anytime he want it now, nonstop, and sleeps with me every night. Why wouldn't he be happy?

I even think that Malik is happy. He's getting help with his drinking addiction, his health is getting better and he lives with his stripper addiction, so now he gets all the lap dances he wants and doesn't even have to leave the house, and it's all free...

OK, OK, OK; I may have gone too far with that. I forgot he's broke, so I wonder if she's happy! LOL! Oh, and by way, why is her name Paris? What you say...

# 14

## After the Affair Love Lesson

$\mathcal{I}$ sit comfortably wrapped in my fluffy white robe in my window seat on this gorgeous Saturday spring morning, thinking and writing in my journal while drinking my favorite hazelnut coffee blend. I gaze out of the window, only to see one of the most perfect sights I could have ever wanted to see in real time. I see Drake and the kids washing the car, running and playing in the water, laughing and enjoying one another just like I imagined in my dreams.

I think back on my life and realize that what I've learned in my spiritual walk with Christ. *Since, I's saved nah!* Is that, no one can make you happy. You have to have joy down on the inside, and with joy comes unconditional love, but you have to know where to find it in order to have it. Knowing how to love and how to receive love is not as easy as it sounds; it's more than just feelings and emotions. It's much deeper than that. I'm taking about true, authentic, unconditional love that gives you joy and peace from the inside out, not just on the surface.

See, the only way you can have the real thing is to first understand that you are loved by God and to love Him back the same way He loves you; which means, you have to obey His commandments, by being obedient to

His Word. Other than that, you will find yourself searching and searching and never finding it or anything close to it.

I didn't love my ex-husband, Malik. I considered him my savior, but unfortunately he was the wrong savior. He wasn't the Savior I know now, the one who saves your soul, and then everything else follows. And believe it or not, I didn't really love Drake, because I didn't know how. For a long time that was just selfish lust, a way for me to get what I wasn't getting from Malik and enjoy being pleasured in the process.

Before I could recognize what true love really is, it first required knowledge and understanding from my Father, the Father who was there all the time; even when I felt abandoned, by my biological father; *my Heavenly Father...*God—was there: loving on me through it all; just waiting on me to love on Him back.

The sad thing is, everybody won't get to know what true love really is, and everybody won't learn how to give it, and that's because they haven't gone to the right source to find the true meaning.

So when I was out there searching, and I finally thought I had found it in Drake, I really didn't know how to receive it or even give it in its fullness: number one, because I was not being obedient to God's word by following his commandments; living in sin and cheating on my husband (regardless of what Malik was or wasn't doing, I had made a commitment to God, a vow, so I should have honored that); number two, because I was splitting myself thin between two men. How could I receive or give love in its fullness when I was giving one man about 40 percent of me and the other one, about 60 percent; and number three, because I hadn't studied it and didn't understand it. But more than that, it was because I didn't love myself and see myself the way God did.

But not me, not anymore; now I understand who I am in Him. I found the real me, who He ordained me to be. And He has taught me what love really is, so now I know how to give it and receive it, because now God lives inside me.

Love comes from the heart and the soul, and those are the places that only God can turn and touch, but you have to let Him in. Once I did that, He taught me how to love myself and how to love others equally.

God has cleaned me up, and He can do the same for anyone, even in the midst of your sin. But you have to open your mouth and your heart and let Him come in and work on what He needs to work on in you.

It took me a long time to get it, but I finally did. I think about all those times, I was praying and asking God to help my situation, and I realize that I never once asked God to forgive me for all my indiscretions. It wasn't until I did that; that God entered into my life. Even in my sin, He opened the right door for me. He even saved me from destruction, both mental and physical.

God loves unconditionally! And even the sin of sins has no room if He's ready to deliver you, but you have to be ready to be delivered as well. You have to want it from the heart, and you have to ask for forgiveness and deliverance all together. You can't just pray for deliverance if you haven't repented. It doesn't work like that. I tried it, and it got me know where, but right back where I started.

See, it's all the trick of the enemy when you're in the world. He'll show you half the story, his story. So that's all you can see. But God will open your eyes to a better story, a story that can last until eternity! Don't think that just because you're in sin that you can't come out. Sometimes the enemy will try to trick up your mind and send bipolar-schizophrenic delusions and mirages to distract you and to tell you that you are not worthy to come out, like he used to do to me.

But even though Drake and I had been obeying and being puppets for the enemy for years, when I asked for forgiveness with all my heart, God stepped in, right in the middle of my sin, while I was in that bathtub drinking wine, having bipolar-schizophrenic delusions, and He took over. Little did I know in that sinful hour God was preparing me for my deliverance. But don't get it twisted; it came with a sacrifice.

Remember when I said that I got awarded the house in the divorce settlement; well a few days later, I found out from my attorney Larry, that I would not be able to keep, or sale the house; unless I was willing to pay out tons of money to the IRS. *Yes, honey!* The IRS had placed a million dollar lean on the house; due to Malik, not paying his business taxes, for over several years.

Luckily this was the house that Malik had built and purchased, before we got married, so the loan was in his name alone and not mine— nor was I on the deed, because if I was; I would have been held liable for paying that money back as well. And the fact, that I had never officially taken Malik's last name as a married couple, and had always filed my taxes separate from his; saved me from being caught up in his IRS mess also. *It's that not crazy? Even in your mess, God still be looking out!*

That said, in order for me to sale the house, I would have had to pay the IRS on behalf of Malik. *No way!* The house wasn't even worth that much, so I told Malik he could keep it. See, that's why Malik was fine with moving out and moving in with his girlfriend, because he knew about the lean all along, and had not mentioned a word of it to me. *Isn't that something?* He was still being slick and sneaky, even in the end. The IRS even wiped our joint bank account clean, before I even had a chance to sign the divorce papers.

But it's OK because the sacrifice was well worth the reconciliation. God reconciled me and everything I had lost, and I will be forever grateful for that. Yeah, I could have fought the IRS for my part of the money but I just let it go. Because when you're done, you're done. And who do you know of, that has ever won a fight against the IRS anyway?

I have been redeemed by God, and all my indiscretions have been placed behind me, thrown into the sea of forgiveness, so if God can forgive me— after all I've done...*That's reward enough for me.*

Drake and I found a beautiful home, where we can grow old and raise our children: in the Soulard area, around the corner, from our favorite market.

We got married on June 2nd. We didn't go with Nyla's tenth anniversary date because we decided we wanted to create our own memories together, not attached to anyone else's.

I'm pregnant with my third child. We've already decided on a name for her. We are going to name her Grace Tzion Grimley. Grace, because even when we were waddling in our sin, God still showed mercy and grace in our lives and in our situation, and has blessed us in the process.

Tzion, because at my darkest hour; I could still see the light over the mountains. And of course Grimley, *because it just sounds good.* I *even* had to represent, in *this* marriage; so I took his last name too. Eva Grimley, sounds good doesn't! LOL!

God has created a union between Drake and me that no man can come in and destroy, not even us. Sin has no room in our lives anymore and no power over this marriage. If it dares to challenge our combined strength, the enemy will only end up losing because God resides all up and in and throughout this right here.

So don't think you are ever so far in your mess that God has turned His back on you. I'm a witness that even in your most grimy sin, if you ask God for forgiveness and mean it from your heart and keep the faith, you can be delivered.

Look at me, look at my story. I never thought I would be saved and sanctified, speaking in tongues, running around preaching like Nyla. Now I'm walking around preaching that same Word to China that Nyla used to be preaching to me, and many others. I'm truly delivered from drinking now, and I've even stopped using bad language. Yes, I ain't said a cuss word, since I cursed Malik out, for not telling me about the lean on the house, and letting the IRS take my money. Yeah, I let it go, but I had to go in on him, before I let it go; that was only right. He was all kind of broke, needy, petty, so-and-so's. LOL!

But, God is awesome in all things; He is awesome and He is faithful, and His Word is true.

You know, Nyla used to always tell me that she and Jamal were praying for me; then she would quote Romans 8:28 to me. *And we know that in all things God works for the good of those who love him, who have been called according to his purpose.*

I would tell her that I appreciated the prayers, but I could never fully understand what the scripture meant or why she would always quote it, but now I do, and it's a wonderful thing.

That scripture is painted on me and Drake's bedroom wall, over our bed to remind us every night, where we came from and how blessed we are to have made it out of our sin, alive.

It's a wonderful thing, to know that you have people who are praying for you, even when you can't pray for yourself. I thank the Lord, for bringing Nyla into my life every day. She was the only thing that kept me spiritually connected to God, after my mother passed; she used to get on my nerves sometimes but now I understand why. And I appreciate her sharing the love of God with me; because without it, I don't know where I would be?

That said, no more Sin City for me and my family. Righteousness is our town!

# Author Bio

My name is Tammy Hinkle-Davis; I am a Christian woman who loves and respects the Lord, and understands that without Him nothing I do on my own could be possible.

I am also the founder and editor in chief of the website Fanzyflaminfro Natural Hair Goddess Real Talk at fanzyflaminfro.com and the owner and creator of Fanzyflaminfro Hair Products.

I'm married to my wonderful God sent husband, Tremont Davis, and we have four beautiful children. Over the years I have written a lot of poetry, articles, and things of that sort, but I've always dreamed of writing a book. But not just any book: a book that would assist in helping someone; believe and trust God for the Savior that He is.

This book is a reflection of the lives of many people who don't understand the purpose and love that God has for them, so they look for it in various arenas. I am so grateful to the Lord for blessing me with this opportunity to share this story, and I pray that this book will meet you right where you are, especially if there is a need for deliverance in your life.

Your sin may not be like Eva's, Malik's, Drake's, or any other character in this book, but sin is sin, and in God's eyes no sin is greater: they are all equal.

We are all human and sometimes we all fall short, but God can repair, replenish, restore and redeem all in one day, if we keep our minds set on Him, ask for forgiveness and believe and trust in His word.

Hebrews 11:6

But without faith it is impossible to please him: for he that cometh to God must believe that he is, and that he is a rewarder of them that diligently seek him.

53150658R00089

Made in the USA
Lexington, KY
26 June 2016